PHANTOM BODIES: THE HUMAN AURA IN ART

Edited by
Mark W. Scala

Essays by
Martha Buskirk
Eleanor Heartney
Lisa Saltzman
Mark W. Scala

Frist Center for the Visual Arts
Nashville, TN

Published by the Frist Center for the Visual Arts
Distributed by Vanderbilt University Press

First printing 2015

This book is printed on acid-free paper.
Printed on Luxo Art Silk
Typeset in Plan Grotesque and Prumo
Manufactured in Spain

Library of Congress Cataloging-in-Publication Data

Phantom bodies : the human aura in art / edited by Mark W. Scala ; essays by Martha Buskirk, Eleanor Heartney, Lisa Saltzman, Mark W. Scala.
pages cm.
Summary: "The third and final volume in the Scala triptych on the human body. The first two were *Paint Made Flesh* and *Fairy Tales*"—Provided by publisher.
Published in conjunction with the exhibition *Phantom Bodies: The Human Aura in Art*, organized by the Frist Center for the Visual Arts, Nashville, Tennessee (fristcenter.org).
Includes bibliographical references.
ISBN 978-0-8265-2089-0 (paperback)
1. Human beings in art—Exhibitions. 2. Mind and body in art—Exhibitions. I. Scala, Mark, editor. II. Buskirk, Martha. Proof? III. Heartney, Eleanor, 1954- Body into spirit. IV. Saltzman, Lisa. Habeas corpus in the museum. V. Scala, Mark. Phantoms and auras. VI. Frist Center for the Visual Arts (Nashville, Tenn.), organizer, host institution. VII. John and Mable Ringling Museum of Art, host institution.
N7625.5.P49 2015
704.9'42—dc23
2015028990

ISBN 978-0-8265-2089-0

Book designer: Beverly Joel, pulp, ink
Copyeditor: Monica Rumsey, Scholarly Editing, Inc.
Managing editor: Wallace Joiner, Frist Center for the Visual Arts

Front cover: Sally Mann. *Time and the Bell*, 2008. Gelatin silver print, edition of 5. Courtesy of the artist and Gagosian Gallery. © Sally Mann. Back cover: Magdalena Abakanowicz. *DYBY*, 1993. Wood, burlap, and resin. Weatherspoon Art Museum, The University of North Carolina at Greensboro, Museum purchase with funds from the Tannenbaum-Sternberger Foundation in honor of Leah Louise Tannenbaum, 2000. Reproduced with permission of the artist

Published in conjunction with the exhibition *Phantom Bodies: The Human Aura in Art*, organized by the Frist Center for the Visual Arts, Nashville, Tennessee (fristcenter.org).

Phantom Bodies is supported in part by grants from the National Endowment for the Arts and the Dedalus Foundation, Inc.

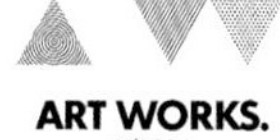

DEDALUS FOUNDATION

The Frist Center gratefully acknowledges the Friends of Contemporary Art.

EXHIBITION ITINERARY

Frist Center for the Visual Arts, Nashville, TN
October 30, 2015–February 14, 2016

The John & Mable Ringling Museum of Art, Sarasota, FL
June 17–September 11, 2016

The Frist Center for the Visual Arts is supported in part by

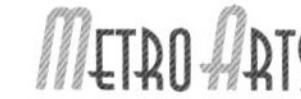

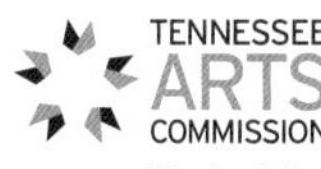

Foreword

The mind-body problem has engaged thinkers as far back as the ancient Greek philosopher Aristotle. How the mind animates the body, the separation of body and spirit, or their interdependence continue to occupy the attention of intellectuals, from philosophers to biophysicists, from the man or woman on the street to poets, visual artists, musicians, and storytellers. The ancient myth of the sculptor Pygmalion and his beloved Galatea is the prime example of the artist's ultimate wish fulfillment, the inanimate object coming to life. What of the spirit gone astray, the body separated from anima, a lingering presence when there is no longer a physical presence?

Chief Curator Mark Scala has been concerned with how artists harness the physicality of the body in art for most of his career. He brings to every project an artist's sensibility and a clear understanding of how materials can conjure both illusion and allusion. At the Frist Center, he has organized numerous exhibitions addressing the body as a site for transformative experiences. In recent years, he has created a trilogy of exhibitions that illustrate the ways artists in the late twentieth and early twenty-first centuries investigate the body. *Phantom Bodies* is the third exhibition in this trilogy, which began with *Paint Made Flesh* (2009) and was followed by *Fairy Tales, Monsters, and the Genetic Imagination* (2012).

The titles of these three exhibitions are largely self-explanatory, but one can only fully appreciate Scala's points by seeing in person the works of art that illustrate his thinking. In each exhibition, we see artists challenging and embracing biology from diverse points of departure. Now, in *Phantom Bodies*, Scala takes us deep into a dialogue with visual artists and scholars on the subjects of where the body begins and ends and how the mind permeates and transcends the defining membranes. The journey is rich and rewarding, and once again, we thank Mark Scala for opening our minds and eyes to poetic realms.

Phantom Bodies brings together thirty-eight artworks or groupings that articulate an absent presence through a variety of means. The exhibition would not be possible without the generosity of the artists and the lenders, who are acknowledged separately in this catalogue. We are extremely grateful to them for making their works available for exhibition at the Frist Center here in Nashville, and subsequently at the John and Mable Ringling Museum of Art, in Sarasota, Florida.

Susan H. Edwards
Executive Director and CEO
Frist Center for the Visual Arts

Acknowledgments

Many curators, galleries and members of their staffs, and studio assistants were helpful in identifying works for this exhibition, providing supporting materials, and facilitating loans. We would like to express our appreciation to our colleagues for their cooperation and generous assistance: Elizabeth Steele Basile and Marie Corboy, Bill Viola Studio, Long Beach, California; Joanne Heyler and Vicki Gambill, The Broad Art Foundation, Santa Monica; Zev Tienfenbach, Cardiff/Miller Studio, Grindrod, British Columbia; Howard Read and Maria Bueno, Cheim & Read, New York; Beverly Adams and Susan Driver, Diane and Bruce Halle Collection, Scottsdale, Arizona; Shear Ozeri, Eileen S. Kaminsky Family Foundation, New York; Putri Tan, Gagosian Gallery, New York; Mary Sabbatino and Dede Young, Galerie Lelong, New York; Caroline Luce and Molly Epstein, Gladstone Gallery, New York; Kerry Brougher, Valerie Fletcher, and Annie Farrar, Hirshhorn Museum and Sculpture Garden, Washington, DC; Tamsen Greene, Michele Amicucci, and Brian McCamley, Jack Shainman Gallery, New York; Stephanie B. Simmons, Jason McCoy Gallery, New York; Amy Cosier, Hiroki Haraguchi, and Leslie Rankow, Lehmann Maupin, New York; Michael Govan, Rebecca Morse, and Amy Wright, Los Angeles County Museum of Art; Luis De Jesus, Luis De Jesus Los Angeles; Ron Warren, Mary Boone Gallery, New York; Agustin Pérez-Rubio, Manuel Olveira, and Koré Escobar, Museo de Arte Contemporáneo de Castilla y León, Spain; Gary Tinterow, Alison de Lima Greene, Mari Carmen Ramírez, and Maggie Williams, Museum of Fine Arts, Houston; Juan Roselione-Valadez, Rubell Family Collection, Miami; Olga Viso, Siri Engberg, and Loren Smith, Walker Art Center, Minneapolis; and Nancy Doll, Xandra Eden, and Elaine D. Gustafson, Weatherspoon Art Museum, University of North Carolina at Greensboro.

The essays in this catalogue enrich the premise of the exhibition in countless ways. We thank Martha Buskirk, Eleanor Heartney, and Lisa Saltzman for their initial enthusiasm for the project and for providing insightful contributions. Vanderbilt University Press is distributing the catalogue and we gratefully acknowledge our colleagues there, especially Michael Ames, executive director. Monica S. Rumsey served as editor, and our appreciation for her careful attention to detail cannot be overstated. The handsome design was provided by Beverly Joel of pulp, ink.

At the Frist Center, we acknowledge the staff who contribute in myriad ways to the production of exhibitions, with particular thanks to Richard Feaster, registrar; Wallace Joiner, managing editor; Michael Brechner, designer; and Phil El Rassi, graphic designer. Interns Margot Danis and Alexander Penn assisted with research, and bilingual visitor services associate Veronica de la Cruz provided invaluable translation services. As chief curator, Mark Scala is the driving force in the exhibitions department. We thank him for another thought-provoking exhibition and for this intelligent catalogue. He constantly reminds us that art is not expendable but rather as vital as a heartbeat.

We are pleased that *Phantom Bodies* will travel to the John and Mable Ringling Museum of Art, Sarasota, Florida. We want to express our sincere appreciation to our colleagues and friends at the Ringling—Steven High, executive director, and Matthew McLendon, curator, Modern and Contemporary Art.

Phantom Bodies was supported in part by grants from the National Endowment for the Arts and the Dedalus Foundation, Inc. We also gratefully acknowledge the Metro Nashville Arts Commission, the Tennessee Arts Commission, and the Frist Center's Friends of Contemporary Art. We also thank the Frist Center Board of Trustees, especially Billy Frist, chairman.

—S. H. E.

Magdalena Abakanowicz
Barry X Ball
Ross Bleckner
Christian Boltanski
Janet Cardiff and George Bures Miller
Adam Fuss
Ken Gonzales-Day
Alicia Henry
Damien Hirst
Shirazeh Houshiary
Anish Kapoor
Elizabeth King
Richard Kizu-Blair
Deborah Luster
Sally Mann
Teresa Margolles
Ana Mendieta
Shirin Neshat
Hermann Nitsch
Gerhard Richter
Doris Salcedo
Annelies Štrba
Bill Viola

Bill Viola Studio
The Broad Art Foundation
Cheim & Read, New York
Danese/Corey Gallery, New York
Mike DePaola, New York
Eileen S. Kaminsky, New York
Estate of Ana Mendieta Collection
Galerie Lelong, New York
Jennifer and Billy Frist
Gagosian Gallery
Gladstone Gallery, New York and Brussels
Diane and Bruce Halle
Hirshhorn Museum and Sculpture Garden, Smithsonian Institution, Washington, DC
Jack Shainman Gallery, New York
James Cohan Gallery
Jason McCoy Gallery
Los Angeles County Museum of Art
Luis De Jesus Los Angeles
Luhring Augustine, New York
Mary Boone Gallery, New York
MUSAC, Museo de Arte Contemporáneo de Castilla y León, Spain
Museum of Fine Arts, Houston
Private Collection, New Jersey
Rubell Family Collection, Miami
Walker Art Center, Minneapolis
Weatherspoon Art Museum, The University of North Carolina at Greensboro

Introduction

Phantoms and Auras

Mark Scala

eople often feel the presence of someone when no one is there. This may be a way of embodying the fear of the unknown, the ghost in the closet. It may be a near-palpable memory of an absent person, triggered by an article of clothing, a photograph, a scent, an old recording. And it can even, at rare times, be a feeling of immanence, of being close to spirit or divinity. Regardless of the source, the sense of presence-in-absence reinforces a need—which seems hard-wired into the psyche—to experience a human essence as it exists outside the body.

This exhibition includes artworks that indicate such presences through surrogates: shadows, imprints, or masks; objects as memento mori; or as other matter or energy. The title is derived from the phenomenon known as the phantom limb syndrome. Those experiencing this perception have lost some part of their bodies but feel it to be still present. While it is a source of sensation and frequently of pain, the phantom limb here symbolizes the weight of absence, the longing to fill the spaces that accrue through life.

Loss, remembrance, and the hope for a residual force that transcends the body have been subjects of art throughout history. In his *Natural History* (77–79 CE), Pliny the Elder writes of the daughter of a potter in Corinth who traced the shadow of her departing lover onto the wall as a way of remembering him. Art historian Victor Stoichita notes that her purpose was to turn the shadow "into a mnemonic aid; of making the absent become present."[1] Symbolically, to depict the one who has gone keeps him home, if only in soulless semblance. But the very emptiness of the image

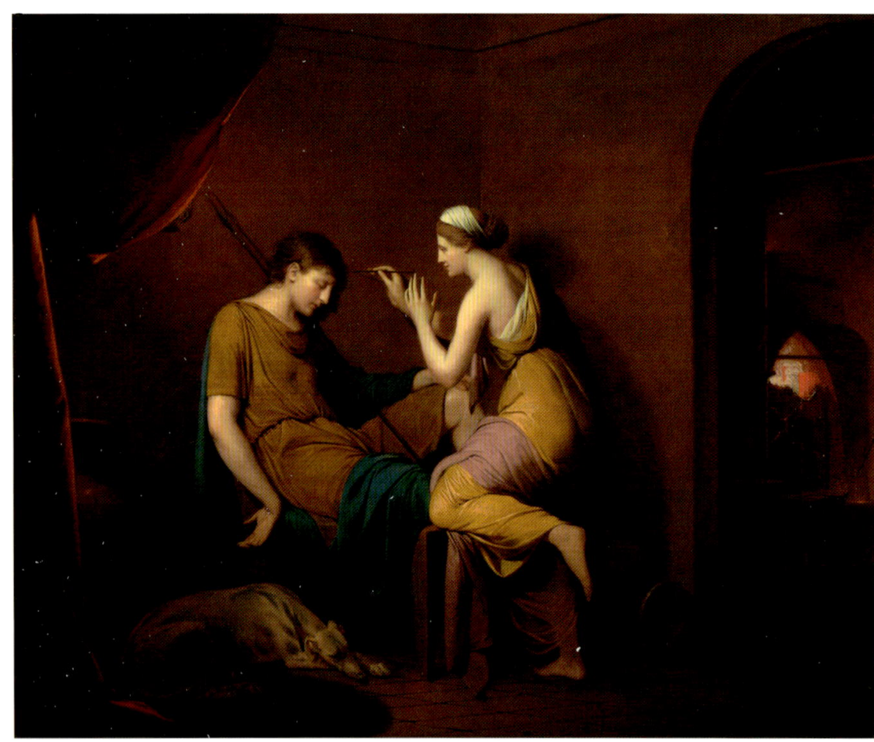

Joseph Wright (British, 1734–1797). *The Corinthian Maid*, 1782–84. Oil on canvas. National Gallery of Art, Paul Mellon Collection, 1983.1.46

inspires yearning and pain, causing tears for the artist and for viewers who may re-enact their own experiences of loss through this image. As James Elkins writes, "Painful absence—whether it is of God, or grace, or just presence itself—is [a] fundamental reason people cry in front of paintings. It is the negative and opposite of painful presence."[2]

How does art cause such feelings? In distinguishing art from other things, Elizabeth Grosz writes that "art is not frivolous, an indulgence or luxury. . . it is the most vital and direct form of impact on and through the body, the generation of vibratory waves, rhythms, that traverse the body and make of the body a link with forces it cannot otherwise perceive and act upon."[3] This constitutes a kind of energy transfer between artist and audience that could be considered auratic; that is, related to the essence or aura. Elkins relates this quality to empathy, a "flow of emotions that merges the viewer and the viewed."[4]

Such a flow is the subject of Barry X Ball's busts of **Envy**, after Giusto Le Court, and **Purity**, after Antonio Corradini (both 2008–12). Ball places them together so that *Envy*, a ravaged old woman, gapes with horror at *Purity*, a ghostly girl. By pairing these otherwise unrelated works, Ball creates a trans-historical contemplation on the subject of death. Whereas Corradini's *Purity* combines chastity and eroticism, in Ball's version, the cloth obliterating her face is more shroud than veil, making the body beneath seem to be an indication of the fleeting nature of life rather than a sign of unattainable desire. The narrative is made more physically pungent by Ball's choice of onyx that has irregular surfaces and impure veins of red oxide and ochre, which suggests transformation and decay. Both figures are corrupt, one with age and ugly emotion, the other with pockmarks and open wounds that eat deeply into the flesh of the corpus. Yet however horrified she may be, the old woman envies this spectral visitor, as if she prefers youthful death to aging decay. PLATE 2

Envy and *Purity* were produced by entering three-dimensional digital scans of the original sculptures into a computerized stone milling machine. After this machine carves the onyx to a close approximation of the prototypes, the details of the sculpture are carved in by hand. With his choice of subject matter and of process, Ball considers the aura as an effect of imagery, while questioning the widely held proposition that a residual human presence can be instilled by the touch of the artist. Walter Benjamin's landmark essay "The Work of Art in the Age of Mechanical Reproduction" explores various dimensions and meanings of art's aura.[5] In his book on Surrealism, *Compulsive Beauty*, Hal Foster breaks down Benjamin's considerations of aura into three principal types: the natural aura, "an empathic moment of human connection to material things. . . . The surrealists were sensitive to this aura of found natural objects, which they often exhibited"; the cultural and historical aura, of both "cultic works of art [and] artisanal objects where the traces of the practiced hand are still evident"; and the aura connected to the "memory of a primal relationship to the body,"[6] which Benjamin attributed to a longing for a return to the maternal body, but may indicate a broader desire to reclaim the sense of well-being once felt in the presence of a protective loved one. In this book and its accompanying exhibition, all of these notions come into play.

A number of the featured artists present or depict objects to posit, like the Surrealists, a special connection to an absent user. The sense of aura rises when we imagine the experience of the missing through knowledge of the artifact's history. That sense is intensified when the history is traumatic. Foster cites the French Surrealist André Breton, who linked aura to trauma in his discussion of

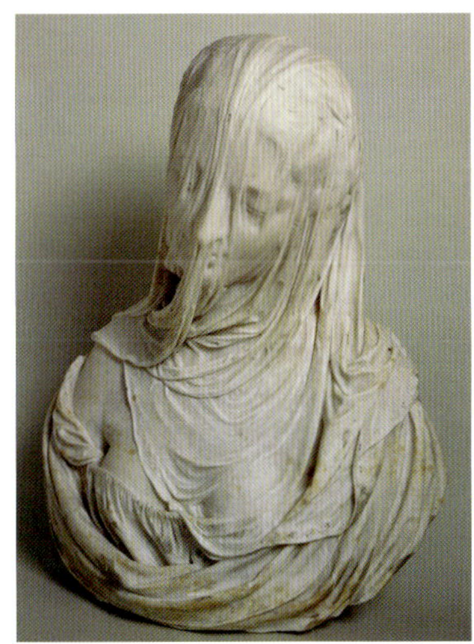

Antonio Corradini (Italian, 1668–1752). *Veiled Girl*, 1717–25. Marble. Ca' Rezzonico, Museo del Settecento Veneziano, Venice. Image: Bridgeman Images

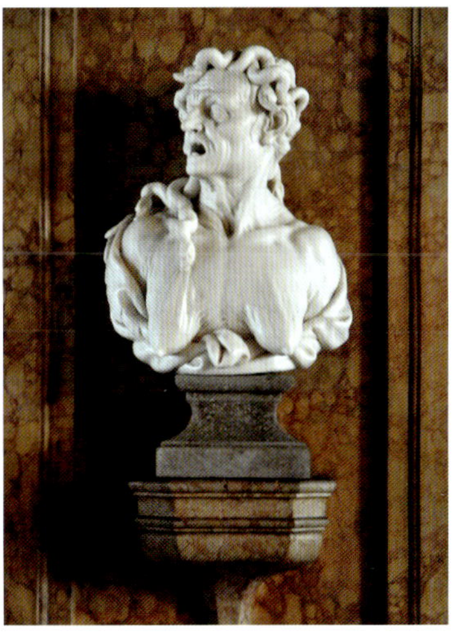

Giusto le Court, also known as Josse de Courte (Flemish or Belgian, 1627–1679). *Envy* (*L'Invidia*), ca. 1670. Marble. Ca' Rezzonico, Venice. Photo: Barry X Ball

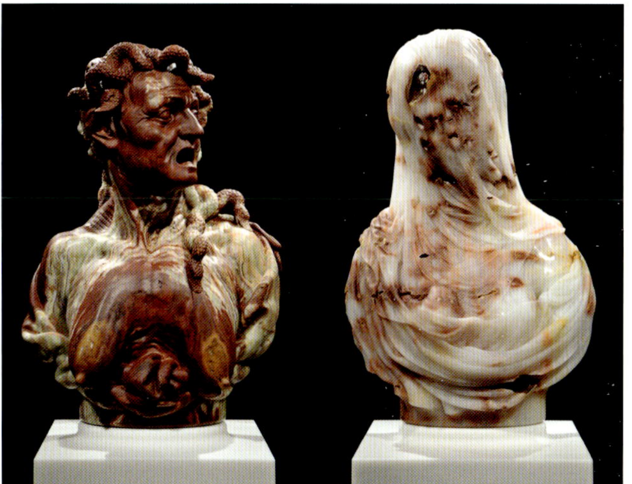

Barry X Ball (American, b. 1955). *Envy / Purity*, 2008–12. *Envy*—Pakistani onyx and stainless steel, *Purity*—Mexican onyx and stainless steel. Courtesy of the artist and Sperone Westwater. © Barry X Ball

Cézanne's painting *The House of the Hanged Man* (1873). For Breton, "aura is somehow involved in trauma, more precisely with the involuntary memory of a traumatic event or repressed condition."[7]

This conjunction often occurs through the agency of the haunted object or its stand-in. Christian Boltanski's **Untitled (Reserve)** (1989) contains reprinted photographs originally taken in 1931 at Chase's High School, a Jewish girls' school in Vienna, whose students were almost certainly persecuted by the Nazis during the next decade. These class portraits are elegies for the persons that were once as we see them, young and innocent. Below, a stack of clothing is a reminder of the clothes stripped from victims in Nazi concentration camps during the Second World War. Boltanski's blurred photographs have been copied and recopied and the clothes did not originally come from the camps, they only represent them. It is up to viewers to make the imaginative transfer required for the work to move them. PLATE 4

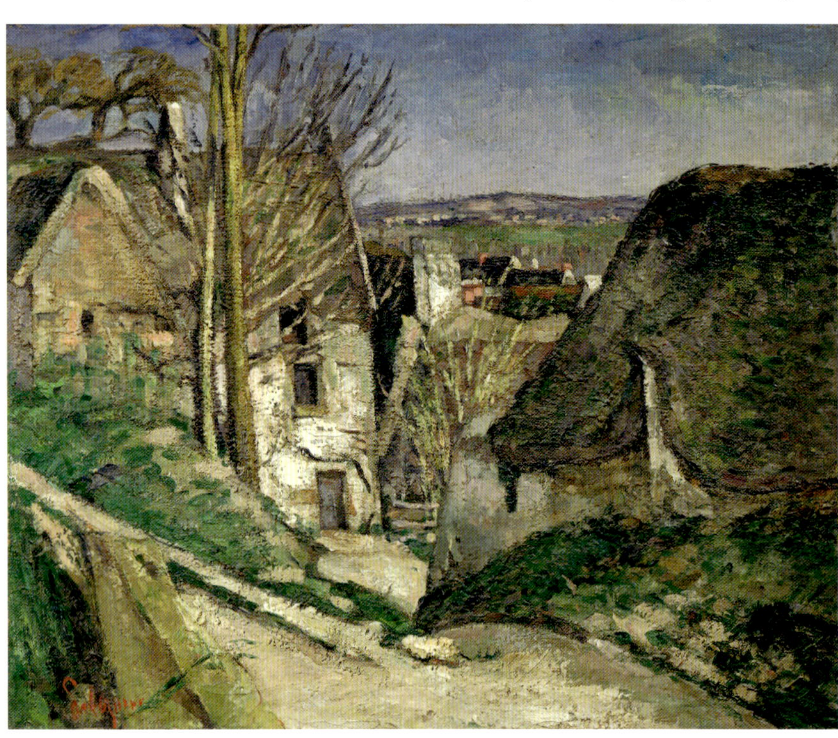

Paul Cézanne (1839–1906). *The House of the Hanged Man*, 1873. Oil on canvas. Musée d'Orsay, Paris, France. Image: Bridgeman Images

Doris Salcedo's **Atrabiliarios** (1992–93), on the other hand, features the actual shoes of people in her native Colombia, South America, who have disappeared as a result of crime or war. Donated by mourning relatives, the shoes are mounted within a wall, as if in a reliquary niche, behind an animal-skin membrane stitched in stiff surgical thread that appears prickly, like an enclosure of thorns. Similarly, Teresa Margolles addresses the invisibility of victims who have died from acts of violence in Mexico. Her **Lote Bravo** (2005) is composed of stacked bricks crafted from sand that Margolles collected in Ciudad Juárez, where the bodies of murdered women have been found. This impassive structure memorializes these women, while it underscores the toll of illicit trafficking of both humans and drugs. The possibility of residual DNA in the bricks adds emotional power, reminding us that many artworks have the blood of the oppressed to thank for their existence. PLATE 39 PLATE 30

In her essay in this catalogue, "Proof? Evocative Objects and Shared Narratives," Martha Buskirk discusses the testimonial power of objects and materials. But she also recognizes that authenticity carries weight. "What proof is there," she asks, "that the shoes Salcedo presents were associated with particular individuals? Their efficacy as material evidence depends on what the artist has told us. Similarly, the fact that Margolles formed bricks using material from specific locations around Ciudad Juárez that are associated with violence against women is not something one is able to read from the objects themselves; yet if the viewer believes her claim, it will powerfully shape his or her reading of the work."[8] This points to the potency of both the relic—the sacred bones of the saint—and the evidence room; DNA cannot be questioned.

Other artists are less concerned with forensics; the object as symbol PLATE 35 is enough. This may be seen in the rose in Shirin Neshat's video **The Fall** (from the PLATES 33–36 series **The Seasons**) (2011), in which each falling petal is another dying child; and in Adam Fuss's daguerreotype of a skull—the most primal signifier of death—or the snake-filled bridal PLATE 8 gown in Fuss's photogram **Medusa** (2010). Such depicted objects belong to the still-life tradition of *vanitas*, the reminder that once-living matter can symbolize the end of all things. Beyond showing fraught objects, film and photographs can, by their very nature, suggest the aura of past lives, moving the recorded subjects, even those long dead, forward to our own moment. In them, we can see the past as simultaneous with the present, linking us to intervening generations who have seen the same films and photographs. This accumulated archive, the phantom memory of culture, includes recorded sound. Music plays a central role in triggering indirect memories in Shirin Neshat's *The Seasons* (2011), a quartet of elegiac films that respond to natural and human-made crises in Africa and PLATE 33 the Middle East.[9] In **Egypt in My Heart**, Neshat shows old footage of an emotional performance by the singer Umm Kulthum, known as the "star of the East," as she sings to a packed concert hall in Cairo in 1965 about time's passing, love, and loss. This footage is superimposed over images of young men and women who participated in the so-called Arab Spring uprisings throughout much of the Middle East from 2010 to 2012, conflating courage, hope, and—in retrospect now that the forces of democratic change have been dampened or destroyed—a keen sense of regret.[10] The words to the song are no less moving than the tone of the singer's voice, and we do not need to know who the young people are to know that their dreams, and often their lives, have been obliterated.

The Arab Spring was a convulsion driven by geographical and historical circumstances, which also provide the background for Neshat's major films, including *Rapture* (1999) and *Women Without Men* (2009). In these films, Neshat conveys ambivalence and sorrow at the restrictions—both in Iran and throughout the Middle East—of religion, political ideology, and unbending traditions, especially regarding the relationship between men and women. *The Seasons* evokes broader cultural traumas, not just affecting the individual but entire populations threatened with repression or extinction through war, famine, or drought. Placing no blame, she only expresses pain and invites empathy. But the viewer cannot help but know that these crises often result from crimes of cruelty, indifference, or intolerance. And we can never call the offender to account, because there is no court of law in which to prosecute an entire culture.

It is the idea of the art exhibition—or any forum in which emotional evidence may be proffered—as courtroom that is discussed in Lisa Saltzman's essay "You May Have the Body. Or You May Not: *Habeas Corpus* in the Museum."[11] Saltzman asks us to think about "art that at once conjures and commemorates atrocious acts and their aftermath, heinous crimes and their consequences."[12] This can be acutely intimate, as she discusses in relation to Janet Cardiff and George Bures Miller's film-noir installation **The Muriel Lake Incident** (1999), in which we are led to believe that PLATE 6 we hear a murder occurring in a theatrical mise-en-scène. Or it can be a sweeping indictment, as in Ken Gonzales-Day's **Erased Lynchings** (2004), showing scenes of PLATE 11 mob violence against Mexicans and African Americans in the West and Midwest, with the victims digitally excised so we concentrate on the perpetrators and the spectators. Both examples question our capacity to know what crimes we have witnessed and to plumb our memories in an effort to provide evidence to others. And both address what the French film theorist Christian Metz called the "off-frame" as a trigger to the imagination: "The character who is off-frame in a photograph . . . will never come into the frame. . . . The spectator has no empirical knowledge of the contents of the off-frame, but at the same time cannot help imagining some off-frame, hallucinating it, dreaming the shape of the emptiness."[13]

The concern with emptiness or absence is implied by the writ of *habeas corpus*, which requires that the custodian or prison official physically produce the prisoner in court to face a trial, so that the court can determine whether the custodian has lawful authority to detain the prisoner. The psychological consequence of making the accused visible is the implicit subject of New Orleans photographer Deborah Luster's series *One Big Self: Prisoners of Louisiana* (1998–2003). These photographs have as their subject inmates at the Louisiana Correctional Institute for Women in St. Gabriel. Luster has photographed them costumed for Halloween or Easter (holidays of transformation and resurrection), thereby concealing their identities. The women's costumes are horrid, as if to magnify their own sense of badness. There is dark humor in the spectacle of criminals dressing like monsters for Halloween. But it is also oddly innocent: children, too, dress like monsters on Halloween. Each sitter contains three identities—the child playing dress-up, the actual incarcerated self, and the assumed persona of evil.

This shifting between mask and self is less dissonant in Elizabeth King's sculptural self-portrait **Pupil** (1987–1990), a homunculus that has the PLATE 19 verisimilitude and finality of a death mask but with open glass eyes that seem to exude consciousness. King, together with director Richard Kizu-Blair, has animated PLATE 18 the figure in the accompanying film **What Happened** (1991; remastered 2008), moving its articulated joints in a graceful way. Its actions are simple—it is filmed in the process of inspecting itself, not narcissistically but more in the manner of the fictional marionette Pinocchio who, at the end of the tale, was surprised to find himself a living boy. In King's piece, there is both correlation and separation between body and mind; she notes that the film's theme emerged as a question: "what does the body involuntarily do when the mind is in motion?"[14] For a split second at the beginning of the video her own face is superimposed over that of the sculpture, momentarily becoming at one with it, to ensure that we do not separate the maker from the made, intelligence from inert material. This aspect reflects the idea of the uncanny, the feeling of uneasy recognition that one may have when encountering a lifeless entity that seems somehow sentient—a double to the human.

The feeling of uncanniness in art occurs when an image of a person seems to have an energy force beyond the capacity of an artist to inject it. Alicia PLATE 14 Henry's spectral figures and masks in **Untitled (Brown, Red, White, and Blue)** (2012–15) have this inexplicable sense of a living presence. Their coarse leather and fabric are like skin and their surfaces are sewn or drawn on in ways that suggest scars, sutures, patched work clothes. Stylized facial features call to mind the visual codes of certain African ritual headpieces and costumes. But Henry's figures have no ceremonial purpose. They are stoic shadows of anger and hurt, resistance and withdrawal.

Like Henry's apparitions, Magdalena Abakanowicz's hollow, head- PLATE 1 less figure **DYBY** (1993) is both bodily imprint and shadow; with no identifiable features, it could have been cast from anyone. The work is a husk of a human, its most idiosyncratic aspect the rough topography of the skin, which makes it seem to have been pulled from the earth. According to the artist, *DYBY* is a Polish word for the "wooden construction used to expose a law-breaker to humiliation."[15] Sitting slightly slumped on a bench, the figure appears to be waiting, perhaps having been isolated to contemplate his or her shame, perhaps for the execution of a sentence. Like much of the work of this artist who lived through Nazi and Soviet occupations in her native Poland, *DYBY* contemplates the spiritually eviscerating impact of political repression. *DYBY* is not a specific victim; rather, Abakanowicz says, it is a "metaphor for the atmosphere of suffering."[16]

Cast by a person or people unknown, the shadow and its correlates, the mask and index, can symbolize universality and anonymity. Each form is a tabula rasa, a blank slate onto which we can imagine ourselves through an act of empathy. PLATE 3 Loosely evoking a magnetic resonance imaging (MRI) scan, Ross Bleckner's **A Brain in the Room** (2012–13) also invites our empathic projection: the depicted brain is someone else's, but it could just as easily have been ours. Just as the MRI translates blood flow and neural activity into areas of gray or pure color, red and blue dots in the painting appear to denote different levels of energy and perhaps the presence of a widely dispersed cellular pathology. Large clusters of blue dots coalesce on each hemisphere of the brain into the bare suggestion of two human figures—uncanny doubles, twins, separated lovers. Unlike a real MRI scan, which shows the convoluted contours of the brain, Bleckner's dots are arranged in a grid, a structure that symbolizes modern, non-hierarchical systems. This implies that any disease recognized in the image refers as much to the macrocosm of rationalist order as to the microcosm of the individual brain.

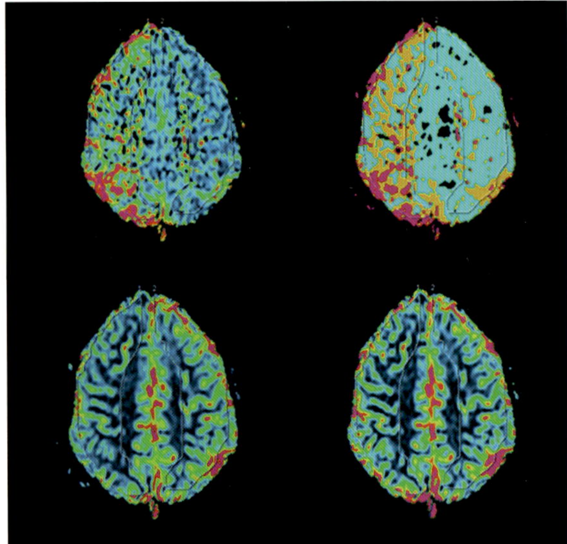

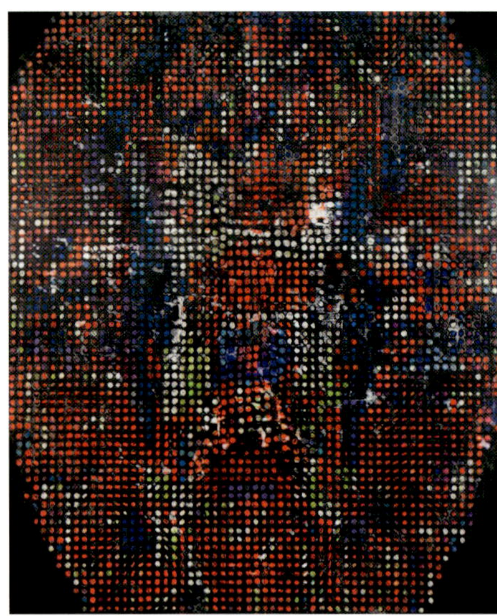

Left: Magnetic resonance brain perfusion maps with region-of-interest measurements of the affected and normal side of an acute migraine attack. Image: Franz A. Fellner, Institute of Radiology, Kepler University Clinic, Linz, Austria

Right: Ross Bleckner (American, b. 1949). *A Brain in the Room*, 2012–13. Oil on linen. Courtesy of Mary Boone Gallery, New York. © Ross Bleckner

Similarly evoking technology intended to give shape to the invisible, the shifting areas of colored light in Ana Mendieta's film **Butterfly** (1975) suggest infrared thermal imaging, which makes visible any variations in radiation through changes in heat. The work hearkens back to early efforts, both of scientists and spirit photographers,[17] to use film and photography to capture invisible human essences and auras. PLATE 31

Acknowledging the thirst for the ineffable that underlay such experiments, Annelies Štrba's video **Frances and the Elves** (2003) responds to the early-twentieth-century fraud of the Cottingley Fairies, photomontages made by young English girls that were believed by many to prove the existence of fairies. More homage than accusation, Štrba translates languid young women into mirages of liquid light, evoking the evanescence of dreams. PLATE 40

According to Pierre Apraxine and Sophie Schmit, some spirit photographers sought to capture life essences that they thought of as "fluids emanating from the medium—the vital force, the soul, and also thoughts, feelings, and dreams."[18] With neither irony nor mysticism, Sally Mann's photographs from her series *Proud Flesh* (2003–09) echo the idea of human essence as liquid. Using the collodion wet-plate process invented in the nineteenth century, she has portrayed her husband's body as it shows the ravages of late-onset muscular dystrophy. This degraded anatomy is recast as luminous shapes, floating marks, bubbles and scratches, and aqueous atmosphere, metaphors for passage from one stage of life to another.

It could be said, even here, that what remains of the self
Unwinds into a vanishing light, and thins like dust, and heads
To a place where knowing and nothing pass into each other,
and through. . . .

Mark Strand, excerpt from "In Memory of Joseph Brodsky,"
from *Blizzard of One*, 2005

In works by Štrba and Mann, the body is softened into atmosphere to mark the movement from being to nothingness. The physical self also dissolves in Shirazeh
PLATE 16 Houshiary's painting **Ode** (2013). Its deep violet space is, paradoxically, also a skin-like enclosure, containing swirling trails of fingerprints, hand drawn with the deliberate repetition of a visual mantra. Just off center is an incision that opens onto a dark and inchoate field. Houshiary provides a metaphor for transition from the intimate to the void: "I looked at the mirror and saw no image of myself. I went very close to the surface of the mirror to see if I could find any reflection. My breath left a residue of mist on the surface of the mirror. I went backward to see if I could see anything. The mist evaporated. I realized this is who we really are—not concrete and not permanent, or definable."[19]

PLATE 17 Anish Kapoor's sculpture **Mother as a Mountain** (1985) finds an equivalent sublimation of the body through color, material, and abstract form. Evoking both a queenly cloak and a mountain, the sculpture has apertures on the angled face that conflate volcanic and vaginal imagery; the powdered red pigment can be read both as lava and the eroded blood of the maternal body.

The corporeal thus redefined as breath, dust, or light is a motif that appears in much lore and literature about the supernatural. It occurs as well in religious symbolism, often as a source of the numinous, the feeling of being in the presence of the sacred. This brings us to artists who impute the possibility of a soul, often through the use of light or other immaterial stand-ins. In Bill Viola's video
PLATE 41 **Isolde's Ascension** (2005), a beam of light plays on the surface of water; the light is suddenly interrupted by the entry of a woman's body—Isolde—arms spread as if in crucifixion. The body rises toward the light as if a soul in ascension. As in many of Viola's works, water and light are here symbols of death and rebirth.

In her essay "Body into Spirit," beginning on page 33, Eleanor Heartney relates this and other works to such religious beliefs as the Christian notion of "the resurrection of the body [and] the Hindu idea of eternal return."[20] Heartney's essay shows her abiding interest in manifestations of religion in contemporary art. While this relationship is often considered irrelevant in today's critical discourse, even the German artist Gerhard Richter—who is renowned for making paintings that appear to have no subject—believes that art still has a spiritual role. For Richter, art can be "the pure realization of religious feeling, capacity for faith, longing for God. . . . The ability to believe is our outstanding quality, and
PLATE 38 only art adequately translates it into reality."[21] Richter's **Abstract Picture (Rhombus)**

(851-1) (1998) interprets the mystical transference of the stigmata, a pattern of wounds from Christ's crucifixion, onto Saint Francis's hands and feet, as a means of making his sanctity visible. *Rhombus*—along with Hermann Nitsch's painting **60 Malaktion MWG** (2011), which conveys the artist's desire to return sacred rituals to modern life; and Damien Hirst's **The Unbearable Lightness of Being** (2003), which links Czech author Milan Kundera's reflection on life's ephemerality to stained-glass windows and Hindu and Buddhist mandalas—shows the capacity of art to find contemporary meaning within religious traditions.

PLATE 37

PLATE 15

All of the artists in *Phantom Bodies* use physical matter to produce a sensation of human absence. It thus seems fitting to end this introduction by circling back to the idea of the phantom limb. After having lost his right arm during a battle, British vice admiral Horatio, Lord Nelson, reported feeling sensations where his arm had been. He proclaimed this to be "direct proof of the existence of a soul." If an arm can survive its own destruction, he reasoned, why not an entire body? [22]

When an arm is lost, there is a body to feel the ghost of the absent member. But where does phantom pain reside when a person is lost; when a family or a community is erased? The question goes beyond medicine to metaphysics, but it may be approached through a clinical example. Neuroscientist V. S. Ramachandran asserts that phantom pain originates in the brain, not in the stump with its severed nerves. He has shown that the brain's surface contains a map of the body's surface. When a limb is amputated, the area mapped to feel its presence is "deprived of sensory inputs it was used to receiving—and bec[omes] hungry for new sensations,"[23] which it invents in the form of phantom feeling. Not just a chart of what exists, the brain map is an active force that reconstructs something that is not there—a kind of bio-mimetic artistry.

In healing phantom pain, Ramachandran has developed ways to interfere, to remap the brain, deceive it, retrain it, to help it adapt to the loss. In thus turning mimesis on its head through therapeutic fabulation, the neurologist provides an analogy that might relate to the role of artists—indeed musicians, writers, any creative person—who similarly interfere with reflexive patterns of living, who alter the culture's nerve center that is always negotiating time and loss, always hungry to be remapped.

Notes

1. Victor I. Stoichita, *A Short History of the Shadow* (London: Reaktion Books, 1997), p. 15.
2. James Elkins, *Pictures & Tears: A History of People Who Have Cried in Front of Paintings* (New York and London: Routledge, 2001), p. 195.
3. Elizabeth Grosz, *Chaos, Territory, Art* (New York: Columbia University Press, 2008), p. 23.
4. Elkins, *Pictures & Tears*, p. 180.
5. In "The Work of Art in the Age of Mechanical Reproduction," Benjamin argues that the cultic aura was a relic of a superstitious past that should be discarded: "for the first time in world history, mechanical reproduction emancipates the work of art from its parasitical dependence on ritual." He also argued that the uniqueness and preciousness of an artwork meant for exhibition, which gave it a special aura and made it a valued commodity for the wealthy, made it ineffective as an agent of social transformation, which was where photography, with its infinite reproducibility, its democratic access, and its capacity to seem objective and thus be persuasive, has an advantage. Benjamin's essay was first published in German in his book *Schriften* [Writings] in 1955. The most recent English-language edition was published as *Illuminations: Essays and Reflections* (New York: Schocken Books, 2013).

Available online at the website *Marxists* (http://www.marxists.org/reference/subject/philosophy/works/ge/benjamin.htm) and the University of Delaware website (http://www.udel.edu/History/suisman/611_S05_webpage/benjamin-work-of-art.pdf).

6. Hal Foster, *Compulsive Beauty* (Cambridge, Mass.: MIT Press, 1993), pp. 195–96.

7. Foster, *Compulsive Beauty*, p. 199.

8. See Martha Buskirk's essay in this book, p. 19.

9. The phrase "indirect memories" describes the sensation of remembering even when we haven't directly experienced what we believe we have remembered. This may be attributed to having seen it depicted elsewhere, to an ancestral vestige, or a memory of something similar.

10. To see this video, go to the *New York Times* website: http://www.nytimes.com/interactive/2011/03/20/opinion/20110320_Opseason_Spring.html.

11. See Saltzman essay, p. 22.

12. See Saltzman essay, p. 27.

13. Christian Metz, "Photography and Fetish," *October* 34 (Autumn 1985): pp. 81–90.

14. Elizabeth King on the making of *What Happened*, from Virginia Commonwealth University's online journal *Blackbird*, posted September 16, 2002: http://www.blackbird.vcu.edu/v1n1/features/king_e_91502/intro.htm. The video is also available on the *Blackbird* website, and on the Bucknell University web page for the Samek Art Museum: http://museum.blogs.bucknell.edu/2012/01/26/what-happened-by-elizabeth-king/.

15. Letter dated July 5, 2000, from Phillip Bruno, director of Marlborough Gallery, New York, to Nancy Doll, director of the Weatherspoon Art Museum at the University of North Carolina at Greensboro, which owns *DYBY*.

16. Ibid.

17. See Eleanor Heartney's discussion of spirit photography in her essay, beginning on p. 33.

18. Pierre Apraxine and Sophie Schmit, "Photography and the Occult," in *The Perfect Medium: Photography and the Occult*, exh. cat., Metropolitan Museum of Art, New York (New Haven and London: Yale University Press, 2004), p. 16.

19. Shirazeh Houshiary, from the audio recording "What is Painting? Contemporary Art from the Collection," artist interview by curator Anne Umland, The Museum of Modern Art, New York, July 7–September 17, 2007. Available online at The Museum of Modern Art website: http://www.moma.org/collection/object.php?object_id=82296.

20. Heartney essay, p. 33.

21. Quoted in Dietmar Elger and Hans-Ulrich Obrist, eds., *Gerhard Richter: Text, Writings, Interviews, and Letters, 1961–2007* (London: Thames and Hudson, 2009), p. 200.

22. Cited in V. S. Ramachandran and W. Hirstein, "The Perception of Phantom Limbs," The D. O. Hebb Lecture. *Brain: A Journal of Neurology* 121 (September 1998): p. 1604. Available online at the Oxford Journals website: http://brain.oxfordjournals.org/content/121/9/1603.full.pdf.

23. See the website for National Public Radio (NPR): http://www.npr.org/2011/02/14/133026897/ v-s-ramachandrans-tales-of-the-tell-tale-brain.

Proof?

Evocative Objects and Shared Narratives

Martha Buskirk

ne underlying premise of *Phantom Bodies* is clearly that the diversity of methods in contemporary art practices has a corollary in the idea that human presence can be evoked via a startling range of strategies. Representational forms rub shoulders with more abstract configurations; references to individual situations open up to considerations of larger historical and cultural forces; and a physical presence can bring to mind a powerful sense of loss. Equally important is the interplay between the particular and the general, evident in the capacity of objects and materials to suggest personal as well as shared histories.

The notion that an object can tell a story has widespread currency. Materials are also linked with specific meanings. Yet it quickly becomes clear that this capacity is not a characteristic of the object in isolation; rather, its power derives from connections to a fabric of human relations, particularly its association with individual or common narratives. When the object in question also happens to be a work of art, one part of its history is likely to include the artist's own account of how it was conceived or brought into being. Yet such origin descriptions are far from the only relevant stories, because a work's significance is constantly being defined on an ongoing basis, in conjunction with responses by members of its audience, who contribute to readings that evolve over time. Matters become more complicated still when an artist incorporates objects, forms, or materials that have distinctive histories independent of their artistic assimilation, since in these instances the viewer may bring associations that are quite divergent from those that motivated the artist. Not only are such objects resonant in their own right, but artistic procedures based on accumulation or assembly also draw power from their connection to acts of collecting in everyday life, including the psychic potency associated with souvenirs or mementos.

Clothing can be particularly charged, implying as it does an absent body. This power is evident in Christian Boltanski's **Untitled (Reserve)** (1989) and Doris Salcedo's **Atrabiliarios** (1992–93), though in some respects their differences are as marked as their similarities. Both make direct or oblique references to historical violence, but where Boltanski evokes the trauma of the Holocaust through his juxtaposition of blurred photographs and folded clothing, Salcedo's work derives from individual histories of loss in the context of Colombian civil wars.

PLATE 4

PLATE 39

Boltanski's references to the Holocaust are part of a larger preoccupation with death. But even when he uses photographic sources where identities could be discovered (school photos, obituary notices), he renders the individuals nameless and therefore anonymous—what was once specific now standing in for a multitude—and he emphasizes this effect by manipulating the images to increase their graininess. In *Untitled* (*Reserve*), the memorialization of loss suggested by the grouping of photographs is echoed and heightened by the rectangular mass of folded clothing below. In another context one might focus on the cheerful profusion of bright colors and prints, but here the accumulation cannot be detached from accounts of German storage depots full of possessions stripped from concentration camp victims and sorted by object type. Nor is Boltanski alone in using accrued mass to invite viewers to think about the traumatic circumstances that may have separated objects from their former owners. A photo of a large pile of shoes at Bergen Belsen in Germany is arresting for its mute evidence of the enormity of such operations in the context of the Nazi concentration camps—and then one knows that those shoes constitute only a small portion of what was found when the camps were liberated at the close of the war. Part of the horrifying power of these objects in Boltanksi's work lies in the recognition that, although they were once associated with distinct individuals, they have since been transformed into an anonymous accumulation.

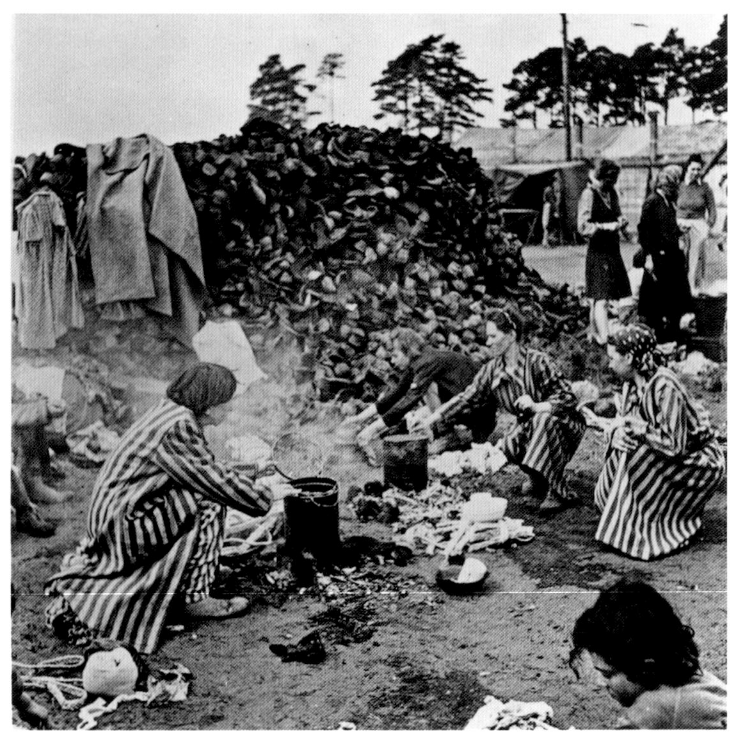

Bergen Belsen, Germany. A pile of shoes that belonged to people who perished in the camp, April 1945. Courtesy of Yad Vashem Photo Archive, Jerusalem

In Joan Didion's memoir *The Year of Magical Thinking* (2005), the author describes how, after her husband's death, she was stopped short in her attempt to give away his shoes by her inability to get around the irrational thought that he will need them when he returns. What Boltanski's approach points to is a certain pivot, where objects associated with a particular person—and perhaps valued because of that connection—are separated, or even wrenched away, from that individual

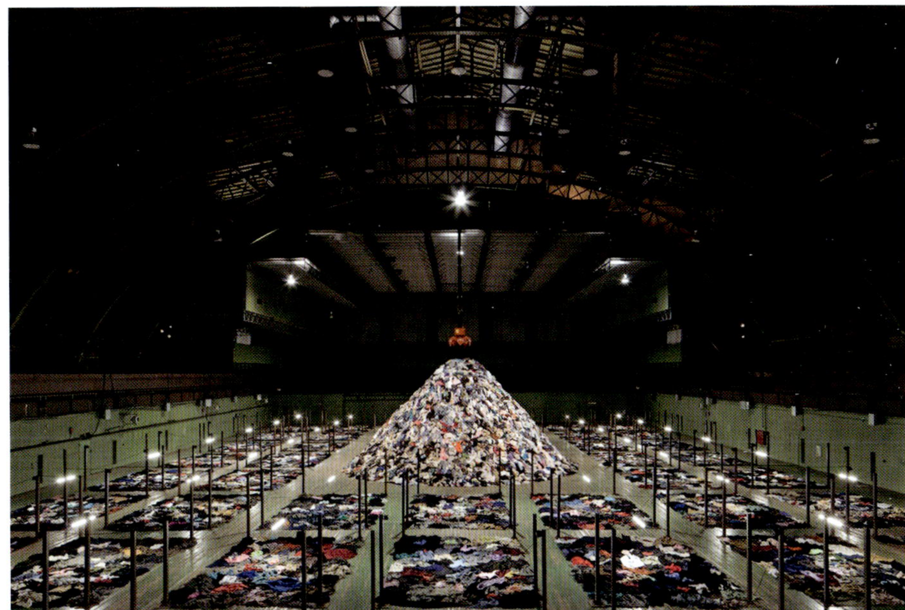

Christian Boltanski (French, b. 1944). *No Man's Land*, installation view at Park Avenue Armory, 2010. Courtesy Park Avenue Armory, New York, and Marian Goodman Gallery. Photo: James Ewing

history. Discussing *No Man's Land* (2010), his massive installation of used clothing at the Park Avenue Armory in New York, Boltanski told an interviewer, "From the beginning of my work to now, somebody and nobody are the same thing."[1] By presenting the material as well as images anonymously, he leaves space for viewers to bring their own set of associations. To the extent that he has acquired these objects from second-hand sources, there is also a very real likelihood that the clothing he is using to evoke ideas of loss or mortality was no longer needed by previous owners for that very reason—but this history is almost impossible to retrieve from the object itself, becoming unknowable as soon as the interpersonal context is lost.

The shoes that Salcedo presents to viewers in her *Atrabiliarios* play into the same set of broader associations, but they are different in their connection to individuals who were "disappeared" in the context of Colombian civil wars. Unlike Didion, who witnessed her husband's death and still could not bring herself to part with his shoes, these families were left with the long-term trauma of not having definite knowledge of the fate of their loved ones. Despite the fact that Salcedo has not given the names of their former wearers, the message here is that each single shoe or pair, isolated in its own niche, stands for someone in particular, with their display giving a form of public voice to private pain.[2] At the same time, however, the shoes seem to recede, becoming partially unknowable as they are separated from the viewer by membranes (made from cows' bladders) that appear to be sutured directly onto the gallery wall. According to Salcedo's own assessment, she provided "a connection between the victims, with their invisible and marginalized experience, and the public which looks at my work."[3] It is important to think about this claim regarding the role of the artist in relation to the structure of the work: Salcedo did not make the shoes themselves; rather, she, like the gallery visitor, comes to them as a witness, and what she has done is to establish the conditions through which these highly charged physical traces are present for the viewer.

The fact that Salcedo used cows' bladders for the partially transparent membranes that encase the shoes in their niches is itself clearly significant, because this animal origin speaks in other ways to mortality. But it is also only one example of the wide range of substances that have entered into contemporary practice—sometimes for visual or technical qualities, but just as often for symbolic connotations. Over the course of art's historical development, certain materials (oil paint, Carrara marble) have been valorized for their visual and technical properties as well as for their associations with the traditions of their use. In the contemporary context, however, the scope of materials and technical methods has expanded exponentially, extending to encompass the highly exotic and the unexpectedly prosaic alike. In the wake of this development, no material can be understood as given, so all choices have to be treated as potentially freighted with significance.

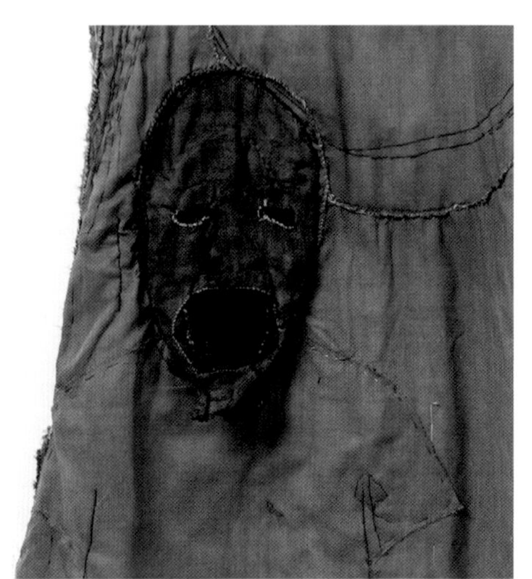

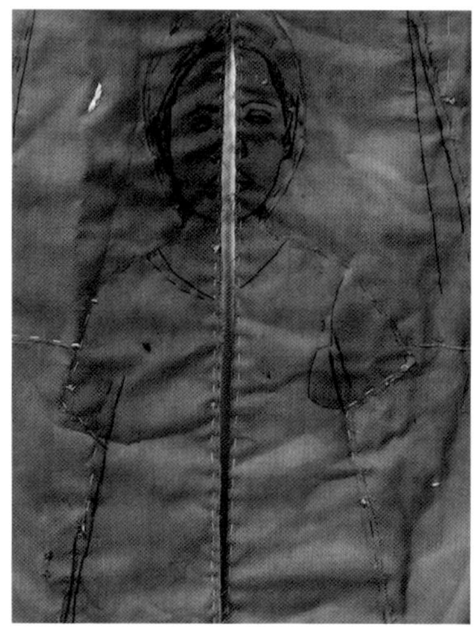

Alicia Henry (American, b. 1966). *Untitled (Brown, Red, White, and Blue)* (details), 2012–15. Mixed media. Courtesy of the artist. © Alicia Henry

Art-historical discourse often treats canvas as a neutral surface and a rectangle as an impartial contour (only non-rectangular examples are described as "shaped" paintings, as if the rectangle were not itself a shape). By departing from the traditional use of stretcher bars as canvas supports and allowing her fabric surfaces to hang more freely on the wall, Alicia Henry exploits tactile associations with the material that she also uses as the ground for drawn and painted depictions. Rather than representing the illusion of skin on this surface, Henry creates forms where the fabric becomes skin-like in itself—an association that is further complicated when the installations also include fragments of clothing (made out of fabrics that do not enjoy the same art-historical privilege as canvas). In the network of relationships she establishes through her installations, she not only suggests connections between people and objects, but she also creates portrait-like forms that have an object-like physical presence.

It is equally striking to see how dramatically a closely appropriated historical form can be redirected by a shift in material nature. In the case of the sculpture **Purity** (2008–12)—Barry X Ball's interpretation of Antonio Corradini's eighteenth-century marble bust of a veiled woman thought to represent this theme—the color and texture of the stone make a dramatic difference. Corradini carved his sculpture from a relatively uniform cream-toned marble. Ball, by contrast, has taken advantage of a high-tech process involving 3-D digital scanning and computer-driven carving to produce his response to Corradini's work in a number of different types of stone. In the version on display here (presented in conjunction with another sculptural bust after Giusto Le Court's seventeenth-century rendition of envy), the original figure is utterly transformed by her presentation in a stone identified by Ball as Mexican onyx, where the folds of the veil are interrupted both by red- and gold-toned veining and by even more disconcerting red-brown voids in the stone that introduce visceral suggestions of corruption or decay.

PLATE 2

As opposed to the stability of stone, or even fabric, Ana Mendieta has used the fragility or ephemerality of her materials to extend the implications of her partially abstract evocations of the body. Mendieta's **Volcano Series no. 2** (1979) explores this theme both through the silhouette shape discernable in the opening to the volcanic mound and in the overall structure, with its intimation of the interior and exterior of the body. Beyond the form itself is the suggestion of the cycles of life, both in the use of fuel that burns away, and by the organic nature of the enclosure. *Volcano Series* was an extension of actions that the artist began the previous year, when she set afire the remains of a hollow tree stump found near the water's edge at Old Man's Creek in Iowa. There she was responding to a site that she continued to visit even as she also allowed it to be reclaimed by the landscape. This work is therefore both a sculptural form and a series of gestures that can be known, in their ephemerality, only through recorded images of the work's transitory existence.

PLATE 32

Given the degree to which artistic deployments of everyday objects and the use of non-traditional materials both have the power to address viewers in unexpected ways, it is striking to see these two strategies come together in works by Teresa Margolles that present moving, complex, but also abstract evocations of loss and mortality. Like Boltanski and Salcedo, Margolles has articulated a pointed yet nuanced response to brutality—in her case, violent crime in Mexico, including the horrifying toll of femicide in Ciudad Juárez. Part of the inspiration for her artistic investigations derived from her own background working in Mexico City's morgue,

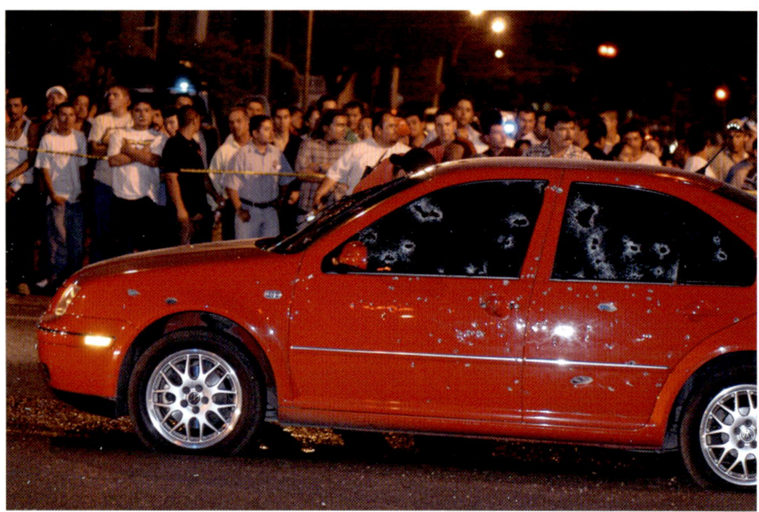

Site of drive-by shooting, Culiacán, Sinaloa, Mexico. Photo: Teresa Margolles

which was connected to her role as the only female founding member of SEMEFO, a performance collective in Mexico City that based its name on the acronym for Servicio Médico Forense, the city's central morgue.[4] Traces or leftovers from that environment have provided the materials for a number of subtly disquieting installations. These have included transforming the water used to wash bodies in preparation for autopsies into an all-encompassing vapor or to soap bubbles, or employing remnants of the threads used to sew up bodies after autopsies to demarcate the space of a room.

Although the two groups of objects by Margolles included in this exhibition and illustrated in this catalogue incorporate equally charged materials, they are less abstract in their initial appearance due to the use of customary configurations. More specifically, these works, which originate in violence to the body, appear in the guise of objects that will have a deceptive familiarity based on their resemblance to traditional forms used to shelter or adorn. The clearly handmade mud bricks that make up Margolles's **Lote Bravo** (2005) present a specific reference to place: each contains sand or dirt that Margolles collected from sites in the area of Ciudad Juárez where corpses of sexually violated women were found. Lurking behind the apparent conventionality of the basic shape (as well as the associations one could make with Minimal Art) lies a highly freighted material trace, although it is one that viewers would not likely discern without information provided by the artist. By contrast, the pieces of gold jewelry that compose her **Ajuste de Cuentas (Score Settling)** (2007) have the look of relatively sophisticated luxury goods. But here, too, direct traces of violence appear in the fact that the broken glass fragments arranged in these gold settings come from car windows shattered during drive-by shootings between vehicles. Opposites are brought together within the pieces of jewelry—but in relation to polarities that already exist in each of the materials themselves: the ugly side of gold is evident not only in its associations with power and privilege but also in the ongoing conditions of exploitation in its mining; while the glass shards, once pressed into the asphalt where they came to rest by passing traffic, have been described as giving the streets a luminous appearance.[5]

PLATE 30

PLATE 29

The disconcerting cacophony of objects and sounds brought together in Janet Cardiff and George Bures Miller's **Exquisite Corpse, enfant** (2012) would seem to relate not so much to the individual works already under discussion, but to the experience of trying to make sense of them in relation to one another. As part of their *Exquisite Corpse* series, the construction certainly evokes the unexpected creatures produced by the Surrealist game of the same name, whereby a piece of paper was folded in such a way that each person had to make his or her contribution

PLATE 5

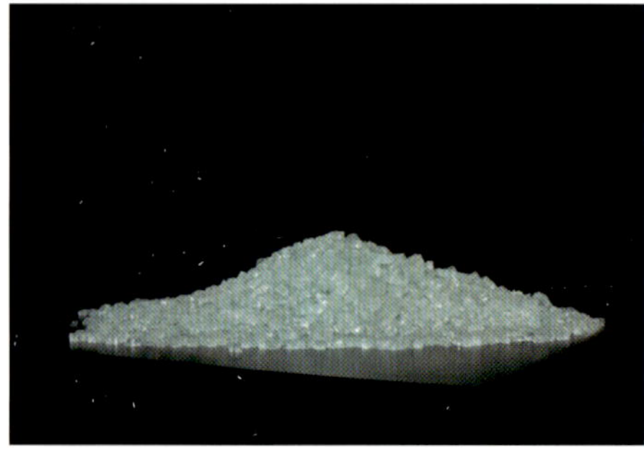

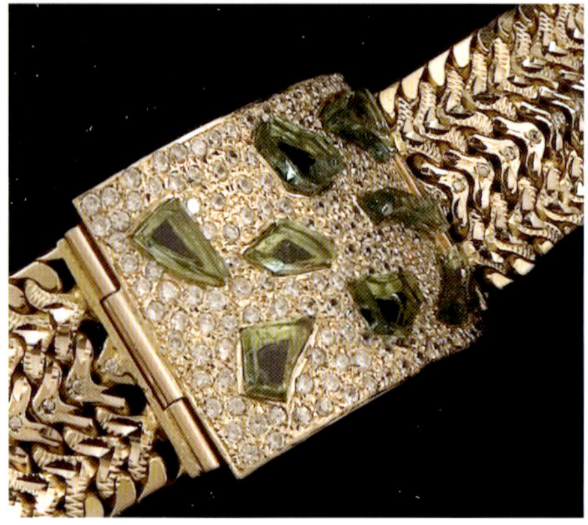

Teresa Margolles (Mexican, b. 1963). *Ajuste de Cuentas (Score Settling)* (details), 2007. 18-karat gold and glass. MUSAC, Museo de Arte Contemporáneo de Castilla y León. © Teresa Margolles

to a collaborative drawing without seeing what had already been delineated by the others. In *Exquisite Corpse, enfant*, the sculptural assembly combines speakers that produce an eerie sound amalgam with a panoply of vision aids, including spectacles and magnifiers that seem to invite close examination. Yet some of the magnification devices do not simply stand on their own but instead reveal objects, including a disembodied eye, that appear to be looking out at the viewer. Thus it is not clear who or what is doing the looking, or being looked at: in a larger sense, the human specter is thereby both implied and displaced, drawing the viewer's attention to the surrounding space and, by extension, to his or her own experience of the world.

Cardiff and Miller's strange assembly asks us, as viewers, to step back and ponder how human presence—or equally important, its absence—is evoked in the works throughout *Phantom Bodies*. One strategy is to represent or abstractly suggest human aspects, thus confronting the embodied viewer with an anthropomorphic entity. Another is to use objects or materials that stand in for an absence. But souvenirs or traces require a larger context. To a certain degree that perspective is supplied by the artist, via information about origins or sources. Yet it also becomes the responsibility of viewers to extend the narrative, filling in the story line based on associations they bring to the work in question.

What proof is there that the shoes Salcedo presents were associated with particular individuals? Their efficacy as physical evidence depends on what the artist has told us. Similarly, the fact that Margolles formed bricks using material from specific locations around Ciudad Juárez that are associated with violence against women is not something one is able to read from the objects themselves; yet if the audience believes her claim, it will powerfully shape readings of the work. The viewing experience therefore neither begins nor ends with the purely visual. Rather, the individual who encounters the work becomes an active participant, connecting the ideas and sensations it generates to frames of reference that extend outward, from solitary experience to shared historical trauma.

Notes

1. See Jan Garden Castro, "Inside the Worlds of the Dead: A Conversation with Christian Boltanski," *Sculpture* 30, no. 3 (April 2011): p. 39.

2. According to Nancy Princenthal, only the first examples from the series used shoes that came directly from victims, while the shoes that Salcedo used as she continued the series were acquired from less specific sources. See "Silence Seen," in Nancy Princenthal, Carlos Basualdo, and Andreas Huyssen, *Doris Salcedo* (London: Phaidon, 2000), p. 49.

3. See Natalia Gutierrez, "Conversation with Doris Salcedo," *Art Nexus* 19 (January–March 1996): p. 48.

4. On this background, see Amy Sara Carroll, "Muerte Sin Fin: Teresa Margolles's Gendered States of Exception," *TDR: The Drama Review* 54, no. 2 (Summer 2010): pp. 102, 107.

5. On the effect of the broken glass, see Rebecca Scott Bray, "Teresa Margolles's Crime Scene Aesthetics," *South Atlantic Quarterly* 110, no. 4 (September 2011): p. 941.

Martha Buskirk is professor of art history and criticism at Montserrat College of Art in Beverly, Massachusetts, where she has taught since 1994. She also held visiting appointments in the History, Theory and Criticism of Architecture and Art program at MIT in 2005 and 2013. Buskirk earned her PhD in art history from City University of New York.

You May Have the Body. Or You May Not

Habeas Corpus in the Museum

Lisa Saltzman

Incident

You are watching a movie, a black-and-white film, equal parts experimental and Western, darkened with a touch of the noir. A bit baffling, the film not only juggles these established genres but also toggles back and forth between two establishing scenes. In the first, there is a woman, alone, in a tight interior shot, piano to her side, dancing slowly, languidly, eyes closed, one strap of her dress, or perhaps just a slip, dangling from her right shoulder. In the second, there is a man, also alone, seated by the shore of a lake, illuminated by a roaring fire, wearing a cowboy hat and methodically cleaning and handling a gun. As the cross-cuts continue, interior to lakefront, woman to man, the camera comes to linger on the campfire. Suddenly, the film catches, stutters, then stops. Within seconds, as if the filmic campfire had ignited the screen, the celluloid melts and bursts into flame, only to give way, seconds later, to an airless, inky darkness out of which erupts, in rapid succession, a sequence of gunshots, each met by increasingly panicked screams from the audience.

What just happened? Were the shots fired on screen or off? In the instant, it is hard to tell. Indeed, even after the chaos has subsided, it remains all but impossible to determine the source of the gunfire, let alone to decipher its significance. But that uncertainty is no doubt quite deliberate. You may have been watching a movie. But that doesn't mean that you have been seated in a traditional theater, comfortably absorbed in the dynamics of a feature film. Instead, you have been standing in a brightly lit gallery space, before a large wooden box, wearing a pair of

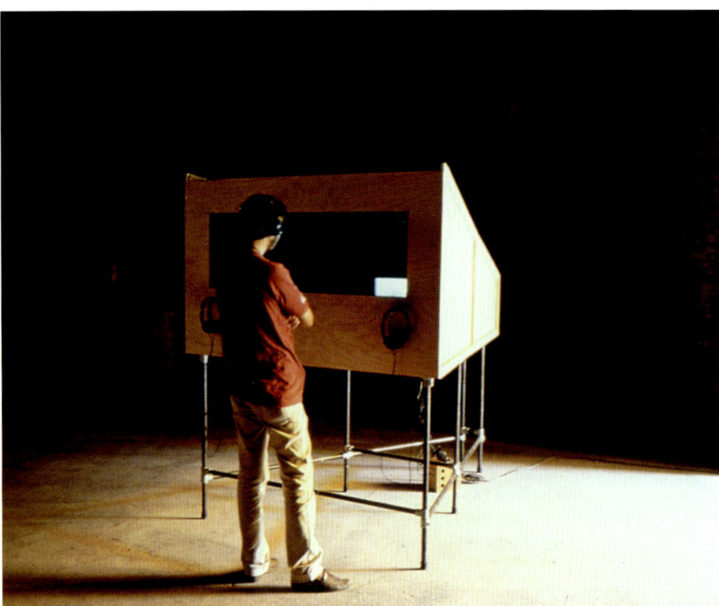

Janet Cardiff (Canadian, b. 1957) and George Bures Miller (Canadian, b. 1960). *The Muriel Lake Incident*, 1999. Wood, binaural audio, video projection, and steel. Courtesy of the artists and Luhring Augustine, New York. © Janet Cardiff and George Bures Miller

headphones and peering through a rectangular portal at a tiny screen—the movie and its surround forming an intricately designed and elaborately engineered work of art.

The piece is Janet Cardiff and George Bures Miller's **The Muriel Lake Incident** (1999). And if the interior of that canted plywood box delivers the remarkable spectacle of an empty movie palace, a Sugimoto in situ, the headphones deliver an even more stunning illusion: a binaural (three-dimensional) recording that captures and reproduces not just the layers of sound from the black-and-white film that animates the tiny screen but also the ambient noise of the theater, delivering the aural impression of an audience whose murmurings and asides are as critical to the immersive sensory experience as whatever ambiguous action first animates the screen. But perhaps most crucial is the resonant sequence of gunshots, which cross—in an extra-diegetic feat, with sound emerging from beyond the confines of the film—from the cinematic realm into the arena of the audience, into your space, an acoustic traversal that punctures the territorial boundary of the narrative and the screen and allows the terror to leak from the filmic world into yours.

PLATE 6

Of course, to have seen *The Muriel Lake Incident* when it was created and first exhibited around the turn of the millennium was not only to marvel at the trompe l'oeil of the perfectly perspectival little movie palace but to revel in the trompe l'oreille, the tricking of the ear, of their wondrously dense and multi-dimensional soundtracks. It was to indulge in those sensory pleasures, to succumb to the pull of those virtual terrors and horrors, a decade before actual gunshots would ring out in an actual movie theater, those bullets turning a midnight screening of Christopher Nolan's *The Dark Knight Rises* (2012) into a scene of chaos and carnage, twelve people dead in Aurora, Colorado, the sudden appearance of the masked gunman, first mistaken for a publicity stunt, all too real.

In the aftermath of that terrible event, *The Muriel Lake Incident* becomes something that it once was not. Indeed, it comes to mean differently—to trigger, by way of inadvertent repetition, the traumatic, even if the piece is but a confection of age-old cinematic conventions and clever auditory and visual fictions. Already laden with portent, the installation becomes at once a prefiguration and a re-staging, at once a premonition and perhaps, even, an unwitting memorial.

All this may seem a lot to pin on what is also, admittedly, an unabashedly playful piece. But even before the events in the Cineplex in Aurora, Colorado, *The Muriel Lake Incident* was also implicated, as a work of art, in a history of malfeasance and crime, violence and its representation. Indeed, it is as if Cardiff and Miller have sutured the unavoidably voyeuristic set-up of Marcel Duchamp's enigmatic crime scene, the violated female body in the disturbing diorama *Given: 1. The Waterfall, 2. Illuminating Gas*. . . (1946–66); the cinematic quest for the fugitive traces of a violent event, as emblematized and enacted in both Michelangelo Antonioni's *Blow-Up* (1966) and Brian De Palma's *Blow Out* (1981). Cardiff and Miller deploy diorama and diegesis, sight and sound, to build on these artistic and cinematic precedents and shift the role of the spectator subtly, irrevocably, to one of witness. But the question remains: witness to what? However disconcerting, even harrowing, the audience experience of *The Muriel Lake Incident* may be, there is only the intimation of a crime. For all the oneiric, dream-like power of the cinematic scenarios and the disembodied voices, for all the terrifying clarity of the gunshots and the screams, when the piece concludes, nothing remains but the empty simulacrum of an old movie palace.

Much more might be (and has been) said of the work.[1] But if certain events, like the shooting in Aurora, Colorado, now infiltrate its allusive armature and amplify its affective impact, so too do certain exhibitions extend its effects as a site and situation of traumatic memory. In this case, *The Muriel Lake Incident* gains further significance by way of its inclusion in the exhibition *Phantom Bodies*, the third in a trilogy of Frist Center exhibitions dedicated to exploring the subject and object of the human body in contemporary art. That body—long absented from a history of modernist painting—was fully re-materialized in the canvases of *Paint Made Flesh* (2009), then wholly re-configured in the mythological and technological hybrid creatures that animated *Fairy Tales, Monsters, and the Genetic Imagination* (2012). Now, in *Phantom Bodies*, that

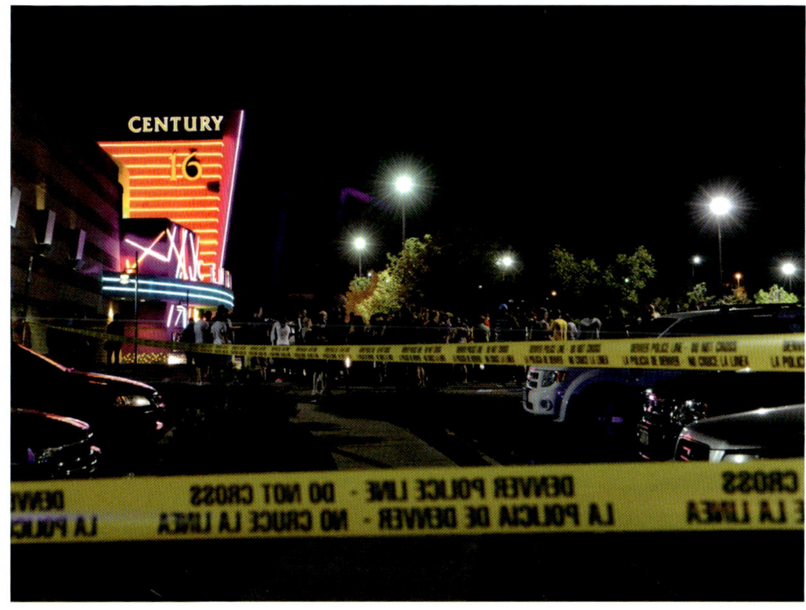

Aurora, Colorado, police rope off the area after responding to the Century 16 movie theater reports of a shooting early Friday morning, July 20, 2012. Courtesy of Karl Gehring / *The Denver Post*

body returns yet again, but this time only obliquely, re-membered almost entirely through its evacuation or erasure, the victim of violations and crimes, injury and injustice summoned almost entirely through its traces, shadows, and ghosts.

Scene of the Crime

Not for nothing have Atget's photographs been likened to those of the scene of a crime. But is not every square inch of our cities the scene of a crime? Every passer-by a culprit? Is it not the task of the photographer—descendant of the augurs and haruspices—to reveal guilt and to point out the guilty in his pictures?

Walter Benjamin, "A Small History of Photography," 1931

Oft-cited, particularly in relation to the eerily empty images of Parisian streets that typify the work of the French photographer Eugène Atget, in all their proto-Surrealism, Benjamin's incisive observation not only insists upon the potential for photography to serve an evidentiary function, and, more to the point, a historical function, but proposes that such intrinsically forensic photographs serve an ethical function, photography not just as index, but as indictment.[2]

Of course, Atget is not Weegee, whose lurid mid-century photographs of murder victims and crime scenes in and around New York City would come to embody something of Benjamin's prophetic words, even if also stripping them of their ethical implications. But perhaps more to the point, indict they may, but these sorts of photographs appear in a museum, not a court of law; they stand as art, not as evidence. That being said, many of the works assembled in *Phantom Bodies* invite us to ask certain questions: How might juridical categories—witness, testimony, evidence, justice—help us to consider aesthetic representation in the present? How, for example, might the writ of *habeas corpus* help us to frame an account of the works gathered in the exhibition *Phantom Bodies*? A writ of *habeas corpus* (literally, "you [must] have the body"), a fundamental tenet of many a legal system (our own included), is a court order that requires that a person under arrest be brought before a judge or into a court of law and, as a structuring legal principle, ensures that a person be released if there is insufficient evidence or cause. Applied loosely to the arena of the art and its exhibition, the writ of *habeas corpus* may help us to approach art that at once conjures and commemorates atrocious acts and their aftermath, heinous crimes and their consequences. Taken together, the works assembled in *Phantom Bodies* bespeak a moment in the arena of contemporary art when the past has become an animating force. Whether that past is understood as "history" or simply as a range of experiences or events, it haunts the present, perhaps nowhere more so than when those experiences or events are traumatic. And it is here—at the juncture of representation and remembrance, history and its inheritance—that aesthetics gives way to ethics, and judgment, that most Kantian of categories, comes to signify far more than taste.

Crimes

Even if we are spared the sight of violated bodies in the photographic work of Ken Gonzales-Day, we know that those absented bodies, in a terrible perversion of justice, were the victims of heinous crimes. First a companion and then a coda to his research into the history of lynching, his photographic series are inseparable from the archival images that are the focus of his scholarly monograph *Lynching in the West: 1850–1935*.[3] His photographic series *Erased Lynchings* (2000–2013) and *Searching for California's Hang Trees* (2013), also known simply as *Hang Trees*, visualized and monumentalized his stunning findings. If his book is revelatory for the ways in which it exposes and documents lynching as a practice that seeps beyond the geographic boundaries of the Deep South and subjects many different people of color to its terrors, it is also stunning as an archive of images.

It is from these archival images that the extensive photographic series *Erased Lynchings* emerges. And if its title describes the process by which Gonzales-Day blocked out the lynched bodies from the photographs, leaving behind only the incriminating evidence of the gawking spectators, it also speaks of the historical elisions that his archival project sought to redress, namely the absence of all those other lynched bodies—Mexican American, Chinese, Native American—from the historical record. In the coda to *Erased Lynchings*, *Hang Trees*,

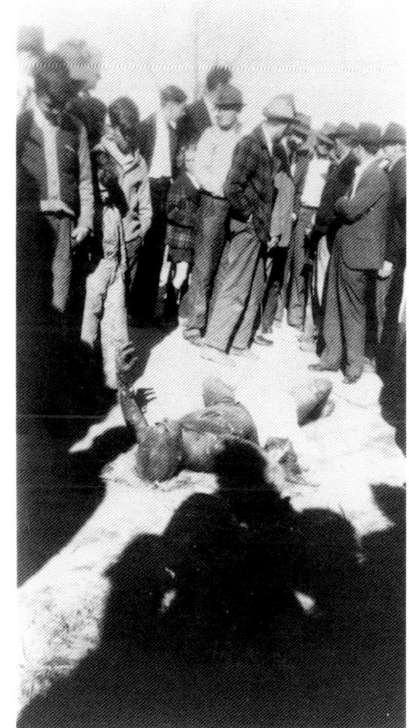

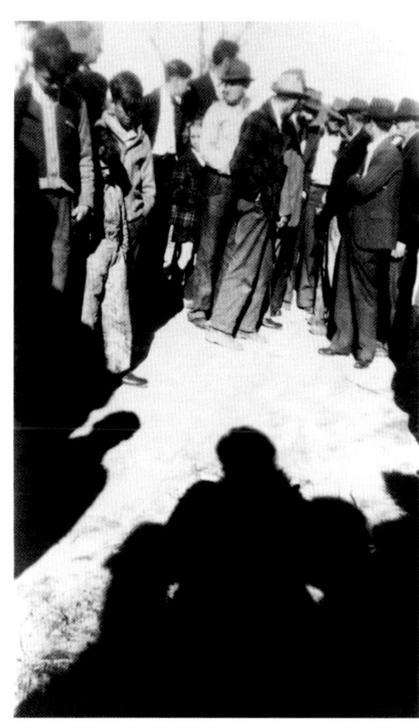

Spectators gathered around the burned body of a lynching victim, possibly Cleo Wright, Sikeston, Missouri, 1942. Gelatin silver print. Library of Congress Prints and Photographs Division, Washington, DC 20540 USA

Ken Gonzales-Day (American, b. 1964). *Sikeston, MO*, 2013. Photograph. Courtesy of the artist and Luis De Jesus Los Angeles. © Ken Gonzales-Day

Gonzales-Day went out into the California landscape, a landscape utterly devoid of any trace of the atrocious crimes that may once have defined and defiled that ground and—searching for their survivors, their mute witnesses—took photographs, portraits of a sort, of gnarled and ancient trees.

But to return to the archival project *Erased Lynchings*, whether taken in such towns as Sikeston, Missouri, or Waco, Texas, or points farther west, the photographs that Gonzales-Day sought and discovered in the archive bear brutal witness not just to the sickening crime of lynching but also to the avid crowds of spectators whose roles as witnesses forever empty that category of its ethical dimensions. Enlarged to ten times the dimensions of the original postcards and souvenirs (a 4-by-6-inch snapshot expands to approximately 40 by 60 inches), the *Erased Lynchings* photographs approach the scale of the kinds of monumental photographs that so often characterize the artistic practice of photography in the present. But where such photographers as Jeff Wall, Stan Douglas, or Gregory Crewdson, for example, stage the scenarios captured, consolidated, and then monumentalized in their vibrant color images, evacuating photography of its evidentiary aspect, Gonzales-Day remains tethered to the archive, to the source image, to the traces of the historical, to the real, even as he intervenes into the image, absenting the lifeless body from its center.

How to consider such pictures of atrocity? Perhaps no critic since Susan Sontag—first in *On Photography*, last in *Regarding the Pain of Others*—has made the case so persuasively, and so poignantly, for the proof the photographic image provides, or at least until Georges Didi-Huberman penned his powerful polemic *Images in Spite of All*.[4] Sontag's *Regarding the Pain of Others* takes readers across a history of images of atrocity, returning to the terrain first covered in her early ruminations on the medium, when, in her essay "In Plato's Cave," she described that moment in her childhood when she first encountered images from the Nazi concentration camps and came to understand the wounding power and ethical complexity of photography, to press even further the ethical question of that belated and mediated form of witness that is the photograph.[5] In *Regarding the Pain of Others*, she turns to a series of "hitherto unknown pictures of horrors long past," the trove of photographs dating from the 1890s to 1930s depicting black victims of lynchings in small towns across the United States.[6] For Sontag, as for the viewers of the New-York Historical Society exhibition *Without Sanctuary* (2000), such photographs were a revelation, not only for the evils of racism they depicted, but also for the inhumanity embodied in the very act of taking pictures of them. The photographs—many showing crowds savoring the spectacles of torture, murder, and degradation—were taken as souvenirs, some even for future use as postcards.

With this historical and theoretical backdrop in mind, I am struck by how adroitly Gonzales-Day navigates the ethical challenge of aesthetic representation in the face of atrocity, yet that deliberate excision of the violated body may be an ethical act in and of itself. In erasing, absenting, refusing the representation of those victimized bodies, he is perhaps protecting them from further violation while still presenting us with the scene of the crime. Harnessing its power to indict, playing on its potential to point (as index) to guilt, Gonzales-Day transforms the evidentiary image into a kind of tribunal where, in the absence of the violated body that can never be redeemed, we stand in judgment before all those complicit in the crime, perpetrators and bystanders both, not only for their failure to intervene, but also for the crime of their all-too-eager gazes.

Memorial

In the beginning, the shoes belonged to the victims. The shoes had aided in the identification of the bodies in the mass graves that Doris Salcedo witnessed, first-hand, when doing research and field work, all to better understand the lives and deaths of the women, the *desparecidos* (the disappeared) of Colombia, her South American homeland. Set within niches in a wall, sealed off but still visible beneath a translucent scrim of animal organs, bladders, stretched taut and sutured to the wall with jagged pieces of surgical thread, the shoes are treated with a dignity denied to the women who once wore them, shielded behind marked and textured surfaces that could fool the eye into thinking they were cracked and aging photographs. At once a wound and a bandage, an incision and a stitch, in their materials and their method, the niches couple violence with repair. And then there are the shoes. For all their anonymity, the shoes counter the oblivion of the mass burial. They and their niches vary in size. Some shoes are dressy, some plain, some elegant, some not. Some appear alone, missing their match, others appear in pairs, whether mis-matched or not. Asserting the singularity of each and every one of the victims, even as they necessarily convey also an irremediable anonymity, Salcedo's installation establishes an aesthetic, an ethic, that is wholly distinct from that so often used to commemorate the victims of atrocity.

Think, for example, of the piles of shoes, toothbrushes, suitcases, and eyeglasses—the utterly useless inventories of objects—that have come to stand, or stand in, for the victims of the Nazi genocide, whether in memorial museums at the death camps in Europe or in Holocaust museums around the globe. Certainly, no artist has exploited that aesthetic more fully than Christian Boltanski, whose assemblages and installations couple the form of the altarpiece with the logic of the reliquary to produce secular shrines to the victims of Fascism, as was first articulated in his series of the late 1980s, *Autels de Lycée Chases* (Altars to Chase's High School). Working from a photograph of the graduating class of a Jewish high school in Vienna in 1931, Boltanski re-photographed each student individually, then enlarged each face until it gave way to the anonymity of blur.

Using a recombinatory logic, he multiplied the images, then arranged them, framed in tin, either individually or in groups, typically above stacks of rusty biscuit tins—sometimes, as in his **Untitled (Reserve)** of 1989, above stacks of children's clothes—memorial as work of art, work of art as memorial. PLATE 4

Salcedo's installation is also an act of mourning, insisting as it does on presence, not absence; memory, not forgetting. But it is also an act of cultural resistance. And so the installation bears the title **Atrabiliarios** (1992–93), which, PLATE 39 though it is typically translated as "defiant," means something far darker and more complex. More fitting would be the rather antiquated "atrabilious"—gloomy, melancholy, ill-tempered—derived as it is from the Latin for a kind of melancholy born of mourning, *atra bilis*, which is itself derived from *atratus*, clothed in black, in mourning; and *bilis*, bile.[7] Of these meanings, Salcedo is fully aware. As she explains:

> There are words that cannot be translated. *Atrabiliarios* is one of those words. It's a word that is no longer in common use; you don't hear it. It's a nineteenth-century word that was used in Colombia to refer to the behavior of people during the civil wars of the nineteenth century. And I was using it in an ambiguous way. It means "people that are defiant" or of that temper. Those words are really weak. This is a very strong word in Spanish—and I was using it both in terms of the ones that had disappeared and the ones that had been disappeared.[8]

Considered untranslatable, *Atrabiliarios* is nevertheless a work that performs something of an act of translation, not so much rendering words from one language to another, but moving something from one place to another, as, for example, the translation of the relics of a saint. And what are the shoes if not relics? By their installation in the gallery, in a museum, the shoes transform the secular into the sacred, the white wall now a repository, a reliquary, a columbarium.

Perpetrators

With Salcedo and Boltanski, we have traveled some distance from the juridical frame. As sites of memory and memorial, their works bear mute witness to the dead and the disappeared. For all the evidentiary traces they marshal to summon their subjects, their project is to commemorate in the context of the museum, not to convict in the courtroom. The closest we come to an indictment is in the work of Gonzales-Day, who—in his exhibitions of photographs—stages something of a belated trial, allowing us to stand in horror and in judgment before all those who enabled the crime of lynching. But whatever the power of his project, that guilt is only assigned retrospectively, all too late to achieve anything we might call justice. Here, as a gesture toward a conclusion, we might consider the work of the American photographer Deborah Luster. Motivated by the brutal murder and irredeemable loss of her mother, Luster embarked on a project that explored violence and its consequences. Working with the poet C. D. Wright, she went into the prisons of Louisiana to document their populations. The project that resulted, an archive of portraits, bears the title *One Big Self: Prisoners of Louisiana* (1998–2003).

In its creation of an archive, Luster's endeavor is something of a repetition of the early criminological project of Alphonse Bertillon, the French police officer who invented the first modern system of criminal identification in his role as director of the Identification Bureau of the Paris Prefecture of Police. The archive Bertillon instituted was structured by a classifying schema that coupled anthropometrics with technology, language and mathematics. An archival project of documenting and classifying criminals, and criminal types, particularly those who were repeat offenders, in Bertillon's system it was the photograph, what we might think of as a mug-shot, that served as "the final conclusive sign in the process of identification."[9] Of course, in terms of a history of criminology, photographs soon gave way to fingerprints as the reigning guarantor of identity. Nevertheless, Bertillon's initiative of using photography to individuate and document a Parisian

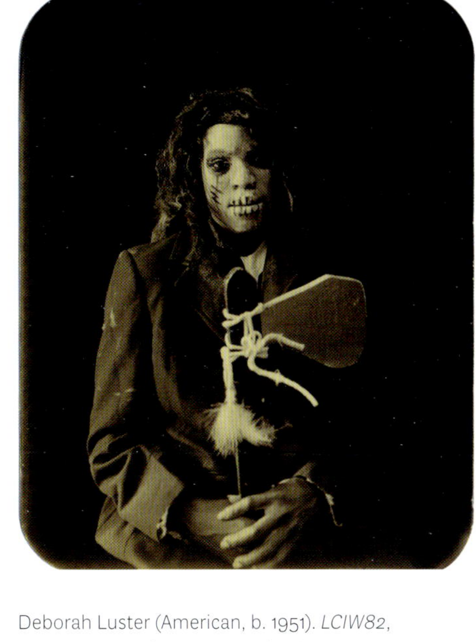

Deborah Luster (American, b. 1951). *LCIW82*, 2000. Gelatin silver print on aluminum. Courtesy of the artist and Jack Shainman Gallery, New York. © Deborah Luster

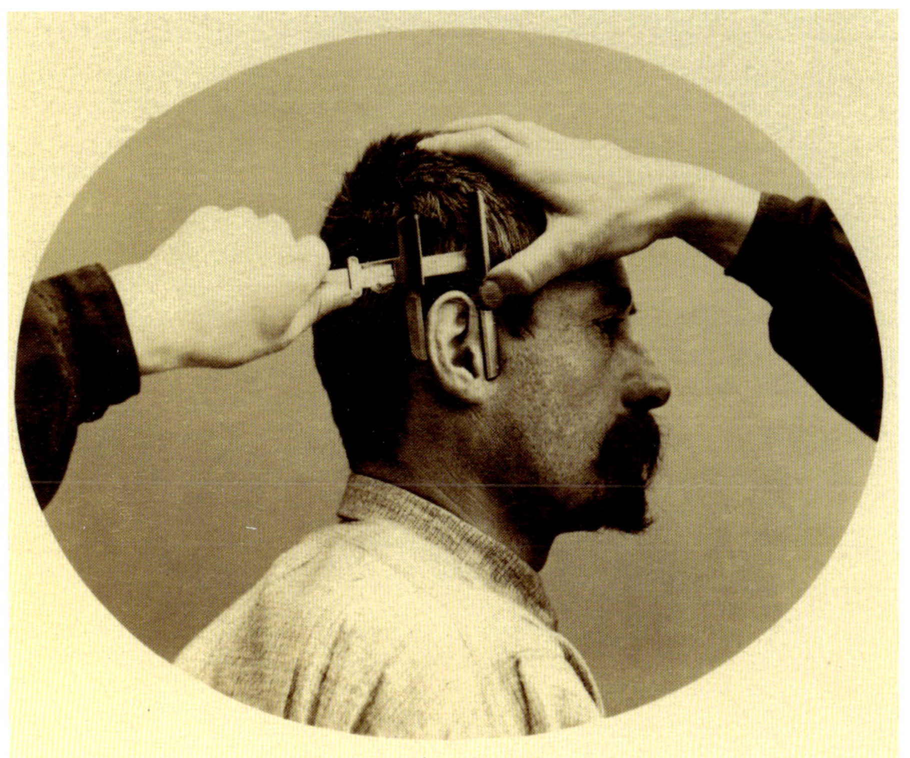

Photographer unknown (19th century). Anthropometric system of Alphonse Bertillon, measurement of the width of the ear, Paris, 1894. Photo: Adoc-photos / Art Resource, NY

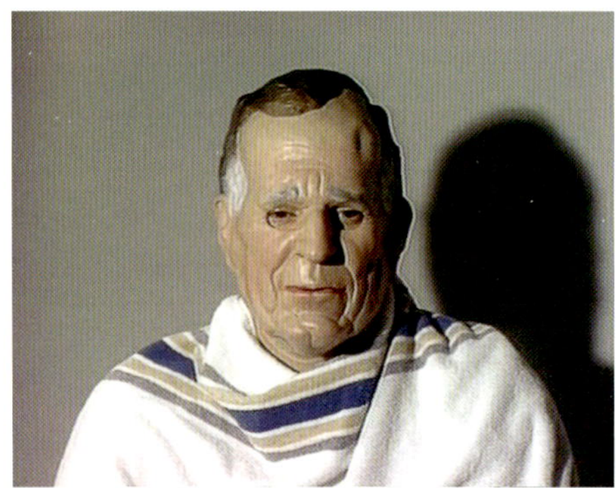

Gillian Wearing. *Confess All On Video. Don't Worry, You Will Be In Disguise. Intrigued? Call Gillian . . .* (film still), 1994. Color video for monitor with sound, 30 minutes. © Gillian Wearing, courtesy Maureen Paley, London

population produced and secured the idea of its evidentiary promise. In short, the photograph, particularly in contexts criminological, came to stand as the emblem and exemplar of proof.[10]

But at least in the case of Luster's series *One Big Self*, we are far from the scene of the crime. That would become the subject of her subsequent series, *Tooth for an Eye* (2011), a photographic archive of sites of homicide around the city of New Orleans. Instead, in *One Big Self*, we are in the realm not of crime but of punishment—or, more to the point—of the punished.[11] Here, the work of the English conceptual artist Gillian Wearing is instructive, particularly given the prevalence of costumes and masks, not just in Luster's prisoner portraits, but in some number of the works included in *Phantom Bodies*. If the mask is a kind of costume that Wearing dons to stage her re-enactments, photographic and filmic, it is also used as a kind of shield, a protective carapace that allows for all orders of confession, from the utterly mundane to the truly monstrous. No such anonymity cloaks or protects the subjects of Luster's prison portraits. Instead, Luster clearly identifies each of her subjects, providing not just, in most instances, their names but also their places and dates of birth, if not also their sentences, their prison work, and the number of children (if they have them) they have left in the outside world. And yet, for all the factual documentation that accompanies each image, the most crucial detail is withheld; namely, the crime for which each prisoner was convicted. True, from the length of the sentence, we might speculate about the crime. But as we gaze at these costumed women (shot during Halloween or Easter), or explore the archive as a whole, certain truths emerge, most obviously, that a disproportionate number of the incarcerated men and women depicted are black. And if the camera bears witness to them, or to anything, it may well be to another injustice, not the crime committed, of which we remain wholly unaware, but instead the exceedingly high rate of re-arrest, conviction, and incarceration that has devastated the African American community in the United States.[12] Subject to sentences stretching months, years, even lifetimes, what, then, of their metaphoric capture, their arrest in the photographic image?

Habeas corpus: you may have the body, or you may not. As the works assembled in *Phantom Bodies* make clear, there are no codes by which to organize aesthetic encounters with the traumatic. But there are precedents. And there is a persistent desire to make sense of the past. Incidents and events, victims and perpetrators, all are summoned through the material object—be it invented or indexical, ephemeral or eternal—that bears their trace. And if *Phantom Bodies* helps us to pull aesthetics closer to categories of justice, we are all well served.

Notes

1. See, for example, Andrew Uroskie, "Siting Cinema," in *Art and the Moving Image: A Critical Reader*, ed. Tanya Leighton (London: Tate, 2008), pp. 386–400.
2. Certainly, this is the premise of Ralph Rugoff's show for the Hammer Museum at UCLA, *Scene of the Crime* (1997), which surveyed thirty-five years of West Coast art to investigate art as a form of evidence and to propose forensics as a form of interpretation.
3. Ken Gonzales-Day, *Lynching in the West: 1850–1935* (Durham, NC: Duke University Press, 2006).
4. See Susan Sontag, *On Photography* (New York: Farrar, Straus and Giroux, 1977), with particular attention to the essay "In Plato's Cave"; *Regarding the Pain of Others* (New York: Farrar, Straus and Giroux, 2003); and Georges Didi-Huberman, *Images in Spite of All: Four Photographs from Auschwitz*, trans. Shane B. Lillis (Chicago and London: University of Chicago Press, 2008). See also the essays gathered in Geoffrey Batchen, Mick Gidley, Nancy K. Miller, and Jay Prosser, eds. *Picturing Atrocity: Photography in Crisis* (London: Reaktion Books, 2012).
5. See Sontag, "In Plato's Cave," pp. 19–20. A pdf file of this essay is available on the website of the University of California, Irvine, SITES@uci: http://sites.uci.edu/01807w14/files/2014/02/SontagSusan_InPlatosCave.pdf.
6. Sontag, *Regarding the Pain of Others*, p. 91.
7. Nancy Princenthal, "Silence Seen," in *Doris Salcedo* (London: Phaidon, 2000), pp. 51–54. For an extensive and penetrating treatment of Salcedo's work, see also Mieke Bal, *Of What One Cannot Speak: Doris Salcedo's Political Art* (Chicago and London: University of Chicago Press, 2010).
8. Doris Salcedo, as featured on the website PBS.org in *art21 (Art of the Twenty-first Century)*, Season 5 (2009), Compassion: http://www.pbs.org/art21/images/doris-salcedo/atrabiliarios-1992-93.
9. See Allan Sekula, "The Body and the Archive," in *The Contest of Meaning: Critical Histories of Photography*, ed. Richard Bolton (Cambridge, Mass.: MIT Press, 1989), p. 358. Sekula's essay first appeared in *October* 39 (Winter 1986): pp. 3–64. For the most recent account of Bertillon's practice, see Josh Ellenbogen's *Reasoned and Unreasoned: The Photography of Bertillon, Galton, and Marey* (University Park: Penn State University Press, 2012).
10. See, among other elaborations of this argument, John Tagg, "The Proof of the Picture," in his *Grounds of Dispute: Art History, Cultural Politics and the Discursive Field* (Minneapolis: University of Minnesota Press, 1992), pp. 97–133.
11. Here we might think of such work as Fiona Tan's all but static video portraits of inmates, *Correction* (2004), or the collaborative photographic portraits of Alyse Emdur, with prisoners posed before images of idyllic landscapes, visiting-room backdrops that give lie to their actual location behind bars. Published as *Prison Landscapes* (London: Four Corners Books, 2013). See also the summary of the book and selected pages on the artist's website: http://www.alyseemdur.com/2_books/index.php.
12. See Alice Goffman, *On the Run: Fugitive Life in an American City* (Chicago and London: University of Chicago Press, 2014), another portrait of a city, in this case Philadelphia, and a generation of young African American men haunted by the specter of incarceration.

Lisa Saltzman is professor and chair of history of art at Bryn Mawr, where she teaches courses in modern and contemporary art. She has been awarded fellowships by the German Academic Exchange Service (DAAD), the Radcliffe Institute of Advanced Study, the Clark Art Institute, and the Guggenheim Foundation. Saltzman earned her PhD in art history from Harvard University.

Body into Spirit

Eleanor Heartney

There are more things in heaven and earth, Horatio, than are dreamt of in your philosophy.

Hamlet to Horatio, from *Hamlet*, act I, scene 5, by William Shakespeare

rom Aristotle to Descartes, a materialist vision of the relationship of body and consciousness has been hardwired into Western thinking. The privileging of physical realities over spiritual ones is the outcome of the supposed triumph of rationalism over woolly "superstition." This vision seeps into our understanding of technology, where the mind-body distinction reappears as the opposition between software and hardware; it encourages contemporary medicine's mechanistic understanding of the body; it denigrates spiritual explanations of physical phenomena; and it underlies the continuing tension between science and faith.

But both traditional religion and contemporary biology suggest an alternate view, instead seeing the material and immaterial realms as inextricably entwined. Birth and death, in particular, mark moments where the complexities of their relationship are thrown into high relief. In the Christian notion of an afterlife which culminates in the resurrection of the body, the Hindu idea of eternal return, and the current scientific speculation about the possibility and ethics of practices like cryogenic preservation, cloning, and reconstitution of long dead organisms from their DNA, we see the outlines of a vision in which consciousness cannot be meaningfully reduced to the workings of physical laws.

This essay examines the various ways in which artists whose work is featured in *Phantom Bodies* challenge oppositions that are variously referred to by the terms body and mind, material and spiritual, matter and energy, science and religion, life and death, interior and exterior. In so doing, the works illustrated in this book and in the exhibition reveal instead the inseparability and interdependence of these essential realms.

Today it is a commonplace to view Modernity as the triumph of reason over the non-rationality of faith-based systems of knowledge. But in fact, the dawn of the modern era coincided with an explosion of interest in Spiritualism, belief in the occult, and exploration of paranormal phenomena such as ghosts, fairies, mesmerism, and telepathy. As confidence in traditional religion was shaken by scientific discoveries and the upending of long-established social arrangements, the boundaries between the invisible and visible worlds began to seem ever more porous. The simultaneous appearance of such new technologies as photography, electromagnetism, and the wireless communication of the telegraph seemed to offer tools which could be used to record and probe otherworldly phenomena (see image at left). In this environment, such figures as the author and physician Arthur Conan Doyle and the American philosopher, psychologist, and physician William James took a scientific approach to the psychic realm, creating experiments meant to prove the persistence of human energy and identity beyond death.

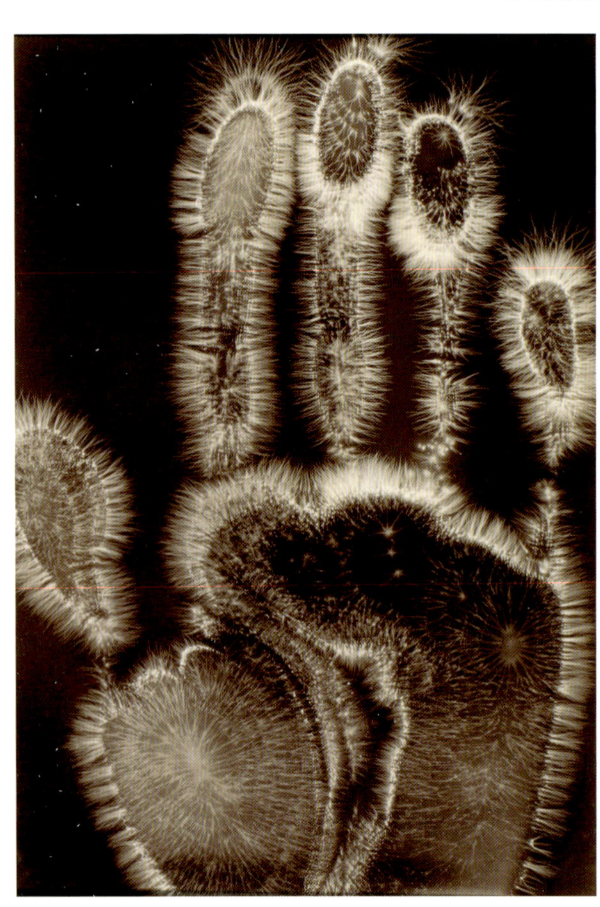

Jakob von Narkiewicz-Jodko (Polish, 1901–1963). Effluvia from an electrified hand resting on a photographic plate, Russia, March 1896. Photo: Adoc-photos / Art Resource, NY

Phantom Bodies includes several artists who draw on now-obsolete or near-obsolete technologies in ways that reveal the power they still hold to uncover otherwise hidden realities. Adam Fuss revives the photogram, a camera-free process that involves placing objects directly on light-sensitive paper to produce a mysterious negative shadow image. Early practitioners of photography such as William Henry Fox Talbot and Anna Atkins put photograms in the service of science, using them to record reverse impressions of natural objects. Later practitioners, among them Man Ray and László Moholy-Nagy, were intrigued by the artistic potential of the photogram and arranged objects on paper to create fantastical and surreal juxtapositions.

Working today, Fuss draws on both of these traditions, employing the process to evoke traces of non-physical energies. He works with objects that have powerful mythic and historical associations, among them rabbit entrails, snakes, butterflies, smoke, and human skulls. In his photograms, these objects are transformed into translucent silhouettes that suggest the continuity of some spiritual essence that transcends physical existence. For one of the images in the exhibition, **Untitled** (2006), he has created a photogram of a baby resting in a shallow tray of water. The image has the quality of an X-ray, with the points where the baby's skin touched the paper appearing as dark masses surrounded by the translucent outline of the baby's body. It's an uncanny image, almost as if the baby is giving birth to itself. Fuss notes that the water here is a metaphor for life and death.[1]

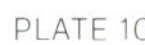

PLATE 10

PLATE 8 Similarly evocative is his **Medusa** (2010), one of a series of works that uses the image of the snake, here appearing as writhing white tendrils within a ghostly Victorian wedding dress. Fuss takes exception to the general perception of snakes, and Medusa herself, that mythic character with hair of snakes, as bearers of evil. Instead, he sees them as affirmations of the life force. In his photograms, snakes resemble sperm, a fact that has bearing on a neglected part of the Medusa myth that relates how her spilled blood generates a golden man and the winged horse Pegasus.

Sally Mann is equally fascinated by obsolete photographic techniques, in particular the collodion wet plate. This is a process that dates from the 1850s in which a pane of glass, coated with a chemical solution, serves as the negative for a photographic image. A relatively long exposure of several seconds makes images susceptible to blurring, a disadvantage that Mann has transformed into an asset. Over the four decades of her career she has explored a variety of themes through dreamy, soft-focus images that seem to come from another time and place.

Mann's photographs tend to be filled with intimations of mortality. Subjects include her children cavorting naked or near-naked like wood nymphs in the Southern landscape where she has lived all her life; empty Civil War battlefields that seem haunted by the lingering spirits of the fallen; oddly poetic details of decaying bodies arranged for forensic study at the Body Farm in Knoxville, Tennessee; and in a series poignantly titled *Proud Flesh*, her husband's once powerful body as it succumbs to the wasting ravages of muscular dystrophy. Mann describes this series as a work of love, embracing the ravages of age and disease that accompany a relationship that has already spanned forty years.

The images in this series recall Susan Sontag's remarks on the relationship of death and photography. According to Sontag, "All photographs are memento mori. To take a photograph is to participate in another person's (or thing's) mortality, vulnerability, mutability. Precisely by slicing out this moment and freezing it, all photographs testify to time's relentless melt."[2] Mann presents fragmentary glimpses of her husband's naked body enveloped in dramatic shifts of light and shadow and overlaid with darkroom distortions. The images emphasize a sense of vulnerability and loss, bringing to mind bits of broken classical statuary still beautiful in their shattered and imperfect state.

Swiss artist Annelies Štrba employs video in a manner that harks back to nineteenth-century spirit photography. Spirit photographers purported to record the auras of ghosts, fairies, and other disembodied spirits. Though later revealed to be frauds, spirit photographs captured the imagination of people seeking solid evidence of a
PLATE 40 world beyond the senses. Štrba's video **Frances and the Elves** (2003) is based on one such sensational deception, which took place in the

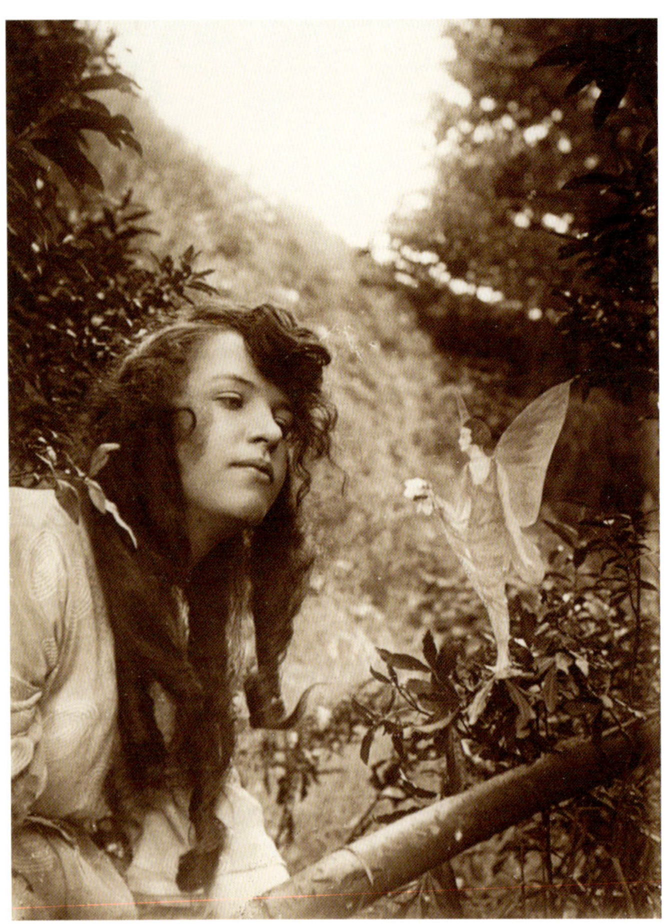

Frances "Alice" Griffiths (British, 1907–1986). Fairy offering flowers to Iris, 1920. © National Museum of Photography, Film & Television / Science & Society Picture Library—All rights reserved. Photo: National Media Museum / Science & Society Picture Library

English village of Cottingley in 1917. Two sisters claimed that they had photographed fairies with their father's camera, and the mysterious, ethereal images of the girls cavorting with tiny winged creatures were not exposed as photomontages until fifty years later.

Like Sally Mann, Štrba employs her own children and grandchildren in works that become meditations on the fantasy lives of children and the fleeting innocence of childhood. Her films and still photographs present digitally altered images of girls who glow with heightened hues of colored light or appear to be melding with nature or rustic rooms and gardens. *Frances and the Elves* is less a narrative than a mood piece, in which the camera follows various young women who glow with unnatural luminescence in bucolic landscapes.

Štrba has acknowledged her debt to Romantic-era traditions in art and literature, citing in particular Emily Brontë's *Wuthering Heights* (1847), a gothic tale that chronicles a love that transcends death. Štrba's own works evoke the sense of a world filled with mysterious presences and half-glimpsed secrets. They remind us of the state of grace extolled by the English Romantic poet William Wordsworth in his ode to childhood: "Heaven lies about us in our infancy" as we arrive upon the earth, "trailing clouds of glory."[3]

Artists like Fuss, Mann, and Štrba channel the fascination felt by early practitioners toward photography's ability to both capture and fabricate hidden realities. One finds a parallel in the apparent magic of today's digital technology, with its creation of an alternative reality that both is and is not "real." Bill Viola, one of the foremost practitioners of contemporary video art, underscores the link between spirituality and virtual reality, noting, "We all have an enormous internal world—it's without limits—and in that way it's like the digital world. Inside your being is infinite. . . ."[4]

His own work draws from a variety of mystical and spiritual traditions, among them Hinduism, Buddhism, Islamic Sufism, and Christianity. A recurring theme is the transformation of consciousness through the union of opposites. Viola has created mesmerizing video works in which figures are slowly consumed by fire or water, are captured floating underwater in a state of dreaming or drowning, or are seen bursting into the air like birds in flight. He has also created works that include videos of his dying mother and the birth of a child, bringing together the two ends of life.

Viola describes **Isolde's Ascension (The Shape of Light in Space After Death)** (2005) as a meditation on the deliberate act of letting go of the body in the last moments before death. Inspired by Richard Wagner's opera *Tristan and* PLATE 41

Isolde, Viola presents Isolde's body draped in shining clothes, rising from the depths in a shaft of light and then disappearing back into darkness as the ray of light dims. Like many of Viola's works, it points to the idea of death not as an end, but as a threshold between realities.

Such blurring of the boundaries between the physical and spiritual worlds is an essential feature of the Christian belief in bodily resurrection. This doctrine, found in Catholic and some Protestant faiths, holds that at the Last Judgment, the dead will be reunited with their earthly bodies to suffer or be blessed for all eternity. Medieval scholar Caroline Walker Bynum has made a detailed study of the paradoxes and complexities involved in this notion of "material continuity" as understood by medieval believers.[5] Its consequences range from strictures about acceptable burial procedures and the veneration of relics consisting of bits of saint's bodies to debates about the status of cannibalized flesh at the End of Days. But Bynum points out that such apparently esoteric dilemmas are not unique to the Middle Ages. In our own time, questions about the meaning of personhood and the continuity of identity after death reappear in science-fiction scenarios about zombies, ghosts, clones, and vampires; in ethical and legal debates over the rights of aborted fetuses and the status of coma patients; and in scientific theories about the possibility of cryogenic resuscitation.

A number of the artists in *Phantom Bodies* create work that contains echoes of Catholic doctrines about death and resurrection. Damien Hirst is best known as a provocateur, mocking the art world with simultaneous international displays of dot paintings or presenting medicine cabinets full of active pharmaceuticals. However, running through his work is a melancholy reflection on mortality that seems to flow from his Catholic upbringing. It can be seen even in some of his most infamous works, for instance, the preserved shark that is, after all, titled *The Impossibility of Death in the Mind of Someone Living* (1991) and his diamond-encrusted human skull, titled *For the Love of God* (2007). Both of these might be seen as contemporary versions of the medieval *vanitas*, a genre of paintings representing death and the transience of life in carefully arranged still-life objects. In this book and its accompanying exhibition,
PLATE 15 Hirst is represented by **The Unbearable Lightness of Being** (2003), a delicate, mandala-like composition made up of real butterfly wings.

Hirst has made a number of works using butterflies, including an installation filled with live butterflies that hatched, fed, mated, and died in the gallery space. Despite the fact that the butterflies lived out their normal life span, Hirst was vilified for this work, which earned him the title "The Pol Pot of Butterflies."[6] The

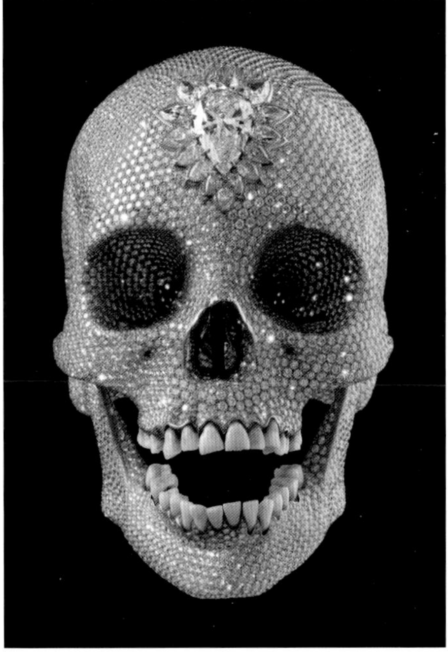

Damien Hirst (British, b. 1965). *For the Love of God*, 2007. Platinum, diamonds, and human teeth, 6⅝ x 5 x 7½ in.
 Photo by Prudence Cuming Associates, Ltd.

work here contains echoes of the Victorian mania for butterfly collecting, but it also speaks about the cultural meaning of the butterfly, whose brief lifespan, iridescent colors, and fluttering flight seem to speak of both beauty and the ephemeral nature of life. Arranged in this seductive mosaic, they seem to speak of a spirit that soars before it flickers, only to live on in the half-life of art.

Such issues are given a more formalist spin in Gerhard Richter's **Abstract Picture (Rhombus) (851-1)** (2008). Richter is known for paintings that oscillate unexpectedly between figuration and abstraction. He creates both painterly soft-focus images drawn from photography and colorful, often abrasive, abstractions that bear no mark of the human hand. He is represented here by a work that is part of a series originally commissioned for a Franciscan church in southern Italy. Richter took as his theme the stigmata of Saint Francis, the miraculous replication on his hands and feet of the bleeding wounds suffered by the crucified Christ. In Catholic hagiography, these marks are demonstrations of Francis's extreme devotion and God's acceptance of his prayers. PLATE 38

The six paintings in this cycle by Richter transform the saintly narrative into abstract compositions whose diamond shape makes reference to the form of the cross and the shape of a person standing with arms outstretched. The rich red and orange hues, meanwhile, allude to blood and flesh. In the end, the commission was rejected, perhaps because Richter's use of the language of modernist abstraction made the paintings unintelligible to the local church authorities. Richter, however, takes issue with such literalism, arguing for a metaphoric understanding of abstraction. He maintains, "Abstract paintings are fictive models that make visible a reality we can neither see nor describe but whose existence we can postulate."[7] Thus, it would seem, abstractions are the ideal vehicles for exploring the religious mysteries surrounding the relationship between flesh and spirit.

With his painting/performance **60 Malaktion MWG** (2011), Hermann Nitsch also creates an analogy between paint and blood and flesh. This work is a natural progression from his more notorious ritualistic works originally staged in the 1960s as part of his Orgies Mysteries Theater. Nitsch's "actions," which deliberately PLATE 37

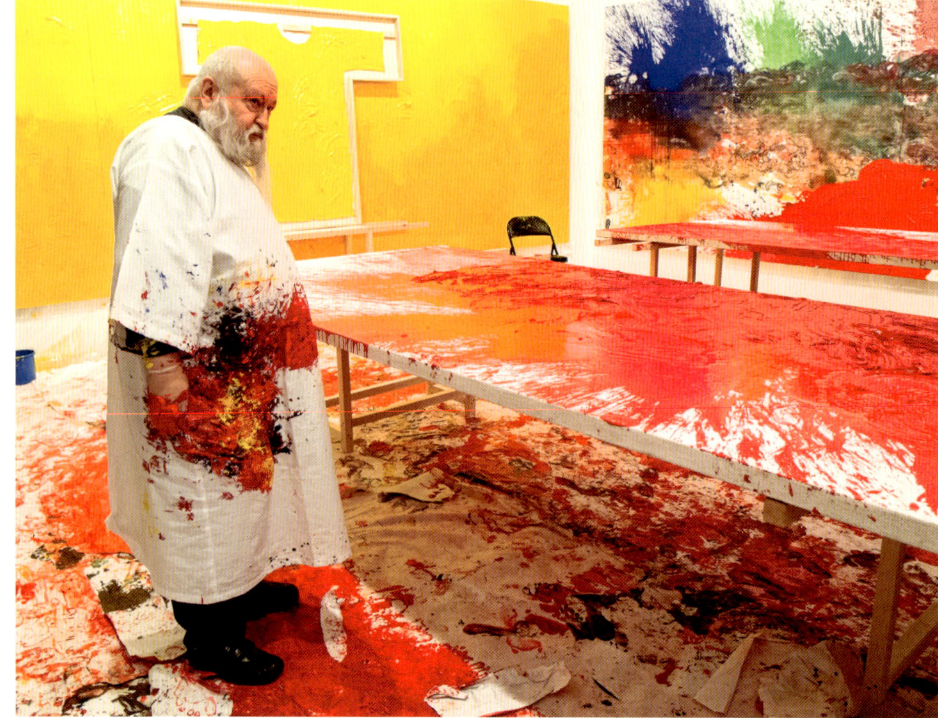

Rainer Hosch (Austrian, b. 1970). Hermann Nitsch performing *60 Malaktion* at Mike Weiss Gallery, New York, 2011. © Rainer Hosch mimed the symbolic blood sacrifice of the Catholic Mass, included the butchering of animals and the pouring of animal blood over participants. In recent years, Nitsch has mellowed somewhat, transitioning from blood to paint in performances that retain the theatrical energy of his early rituals.

For *60 Malaktion MWG,* Nitsch and his assistants splattered, poured, smeared, and brushed paint onto canvases over the course of two days, before a live audience. The transition from body fluids to paint did little to diminish the sense of visceral abandon as participants walked barefoot over pools of viscous paint in white robes that grew increasingly stained and spattered as the event wore on. The canvases themselves, awash with spills and splashes of pure color, outlive the event. They retain traces of the ritual energy that went into their making in a manner analogous to the sparks of divine spirit that, according to medieval Christians, adhered to bits of flesh and bone of martyred saints.

Belief in the permeability of flesh and spirit is not limited to the Judeo-Christian tradition. However, nonwestern spiritual traditions are often less focused on death than on birth as the moment of passage between heaven and earth. An emphasis on generativity and fertility can result in a more female-inflected spirituality. This is evident in the work of Anish Kapoor. The child of an irreligious Hindu and an Iraqi Jew, Kapoor was raised in India in an English-speaking household before moving to London as a young adult. An adherent of Buddhism, his work is as culturally mixed as his biography. He draws on the Buddhist concept of the void, Hindu and Western origin myths, and Romantic-era notions of the sublime to create works that evoke the slippage between the visible and invisible worlds.

Kapoor employs materials and forms that create an immersive experience. These include the application of velvety pigments to natural surfaces to create indentations that swallow the light, creating an illusion of infinite depth; the fashioning of gently curving stainless-steel forms that fold the viewers' reflection into a distorted vision of the surrounding environment; and the manipulation of smoke as a metaphor for spiritual ascension. He uses pure, unadulterated colors, a vital part of his artistic language, for their symbolic meanings. In his lexicon, yellow denotes passion; blue, the godly aspects of reality; and red as an evocation of earth and blood.

Mother as a Mountain (1985) is a work that touches on one of Kapoor's primary themes: the celebration of birth and origin. Kapoor notes that he adheres to an Eastern conception of creativity as a feminine energy, as opposed to the more phallic orientation of Western Modernism. Here, this idea is translated into an open crimson form that suggests at once a volcano, an empty cape, a vagina, and a womb. As the title suggests, it becomes a meditation on archetypal notions of Mother Earth as the origin of all human and non-human life. PLATE 17

Drawing on a completely different set of spiritual traditions, Ana Mendieta has also explored myths of origin. Her works play with her dual allegiance as a Cuban-born American artist to pre-Columbian and Afro Cuban beliefs. She is best known for her *siluetas,* works in which she merged her body with nature—either literally, by lying naked in various landscapes; or figuratively, by creating silhouettes of her body out of such natural materials as flowers, rocks, blood, twigs, earth, or fire. In keeping with her animist leanings, she saw her *siluetas* as simultaneously wombs and graves, expressing her sense of the cyclical nature of life in which death is a beginning rather than an end. Mendieta's **Butterfly** (1975) emphasizes the interchangeability of matter and spirit. In the video, she manipulated images of herself with distortions and vibrant color changes that suggest a figure dissolving into light and energy. PLATE 31

The work of Iranian-born Shirazeh Houshiary also expresses the duality of existence and non-existence. In her mesmerizing paintings and drawings, Houshiary employs the metaphor of the veil as the skin that separates the human interior from its exterior. She draws on her belief in Sufism, an esoteric branch of Islam that centers on the quest for self-knowledge and is based on a belief in the fundamental unity of the physical and spiritual realms. Many of her works are inscribed with the Arabic words for "I am" and "I am not," repeated over and over in a tiny script that transforms them into an all but unreadable silvery cloud that seems to float on the surface of the canvas. In her other works she uses filigree marks, vaporous handprints, or even, in the case of her animations, emanations of human breath, to simultaneously suggest inside and outside, presence and void, microscopic and macroscopic realities.

In paintings like **Ode** (2013), Houshiary calls upon what she refers to as our "dark senses," by which she means those that do not rely on vision. She notes that she wants to create the sensation of human touch, transcending the opticality of much Western work to involve the whole body. The rippling surface of this work seems to vibrate with otherwise invisible energy, as if to form a conduit between the material and spiritual worlds. PLATE 16

Shirazeh Houshiary (Iranian, b. 1955). *Ode* (detail), 2013. Pencil, pigments, and black Aquacryl on canvas and aluminum. Private Collection. © Shirazeh Houshiary

Drawing on a wide range of cultural, historical, and personal influences, each of these artists addresses the Western "mind / body problem" in a different way. Their work attests to the failure of materialistic philosophies to satisfy the human quest for meaning. Instead, they point the way to the richer understandings that unfold when mind and body are seen as parts of a single whole.

Notes

1. "Adam Fuss in His Own Words," *Art on Paper* (September–October 2002): p. 70.
2. Susan Sontag, *On Photography* (New York: Farrar, Straus and Giroux, 1977), p. 15.
3. William Wordsworth, "Intimations of Immortality," 1802.
4. Quoted in Jan Dalley, "Submerged in hidden depths," *Financial Times*, June 7, 2013.
5. See Caroline Walker Bynum, "Material Continuity, Personal Survival and the Resurrection of the Body: A Scholastic Discussion in Its Medieval and Modern Contexts," in *Fragmentation and Redemption: Essays on Gender and the Human Body in Medieval Religion*, pp. 239–99 (New York: Zone Books, 1991).
6. See Alan Van, "Damien Hirst's 'In and Out of Love' Art Exhibit is Butterfly Hiroshima," on the website NMR (New Media Rockstars), posted October 19, 2012: http://newmediarockstars.com/2012/10/damien-hirsts-in-and-out-of-love-art-exhibit-is-butterfly-hiroshima-video/#sthash.pfo8sTqI.dpuf.
7. Quoted in Robert Storr, *Gerhard Richter: Forty Years of Painting* (New York: Museum of Modern Art, 2002), p. 306.

Eleanor Heartney is a contributing editor to *Art in America* and *Artpress* and has written extensively on contemporary art issues for *ARTnews*, *Art and Auction*, *New Art Examiner*, the *New York Times*, the *Washington Post*, and other publications. In 2008 she was honored by the French government as a Chevalier dans l'Ordre des Arts et des Lettres. She received the College Art Association's Frank Jewett Mather Award for distinction in art criticism in 1992.

PLATE 1 **Magdalena Abakanowicz**, *DYBY*, 1993

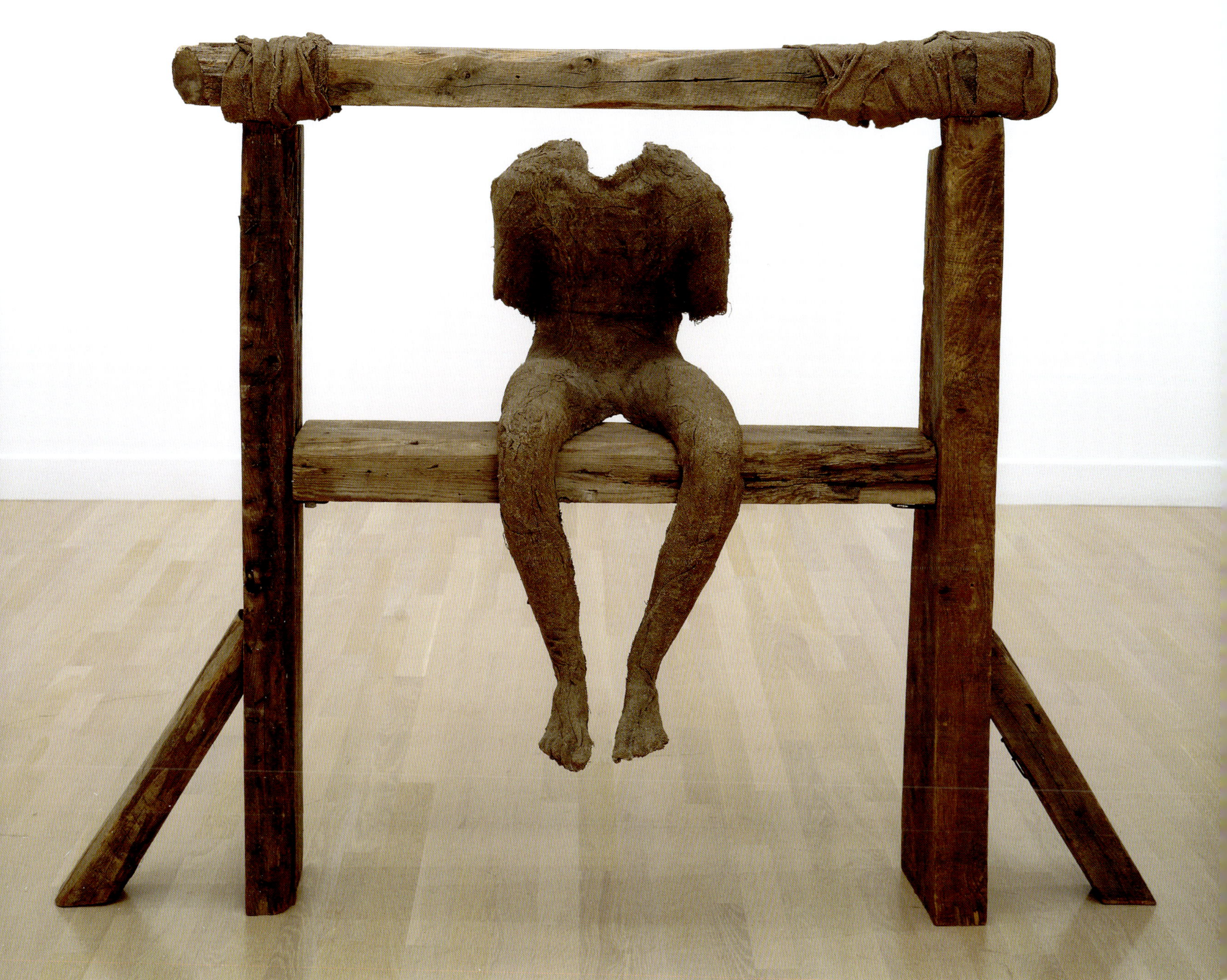

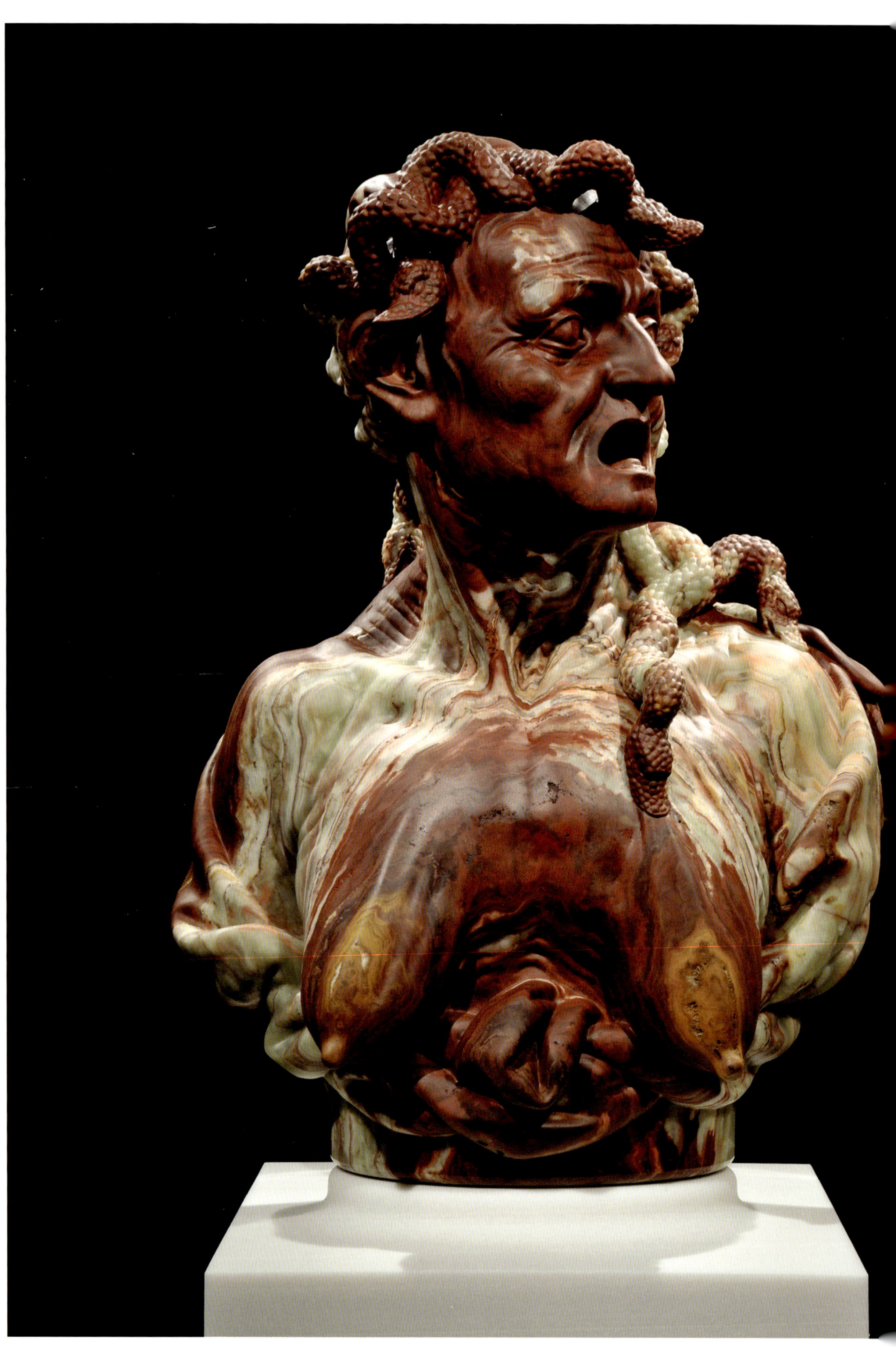

PLATE 2 **Barry X Ball**, *Envy / Purity*, 2008–12

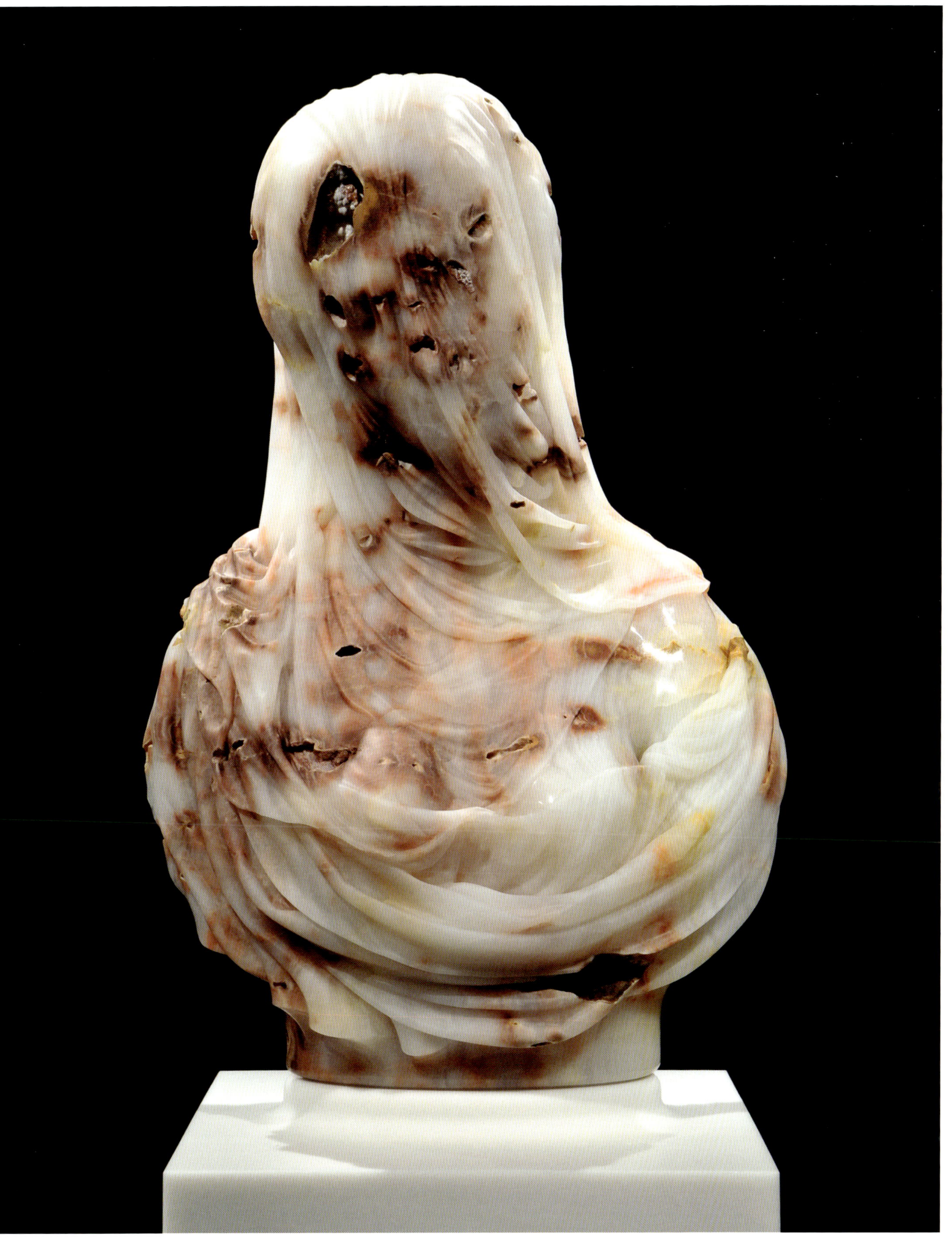

PLATE 3 **Ross Bleckner**, *A Brain in the Room*, 2012–13

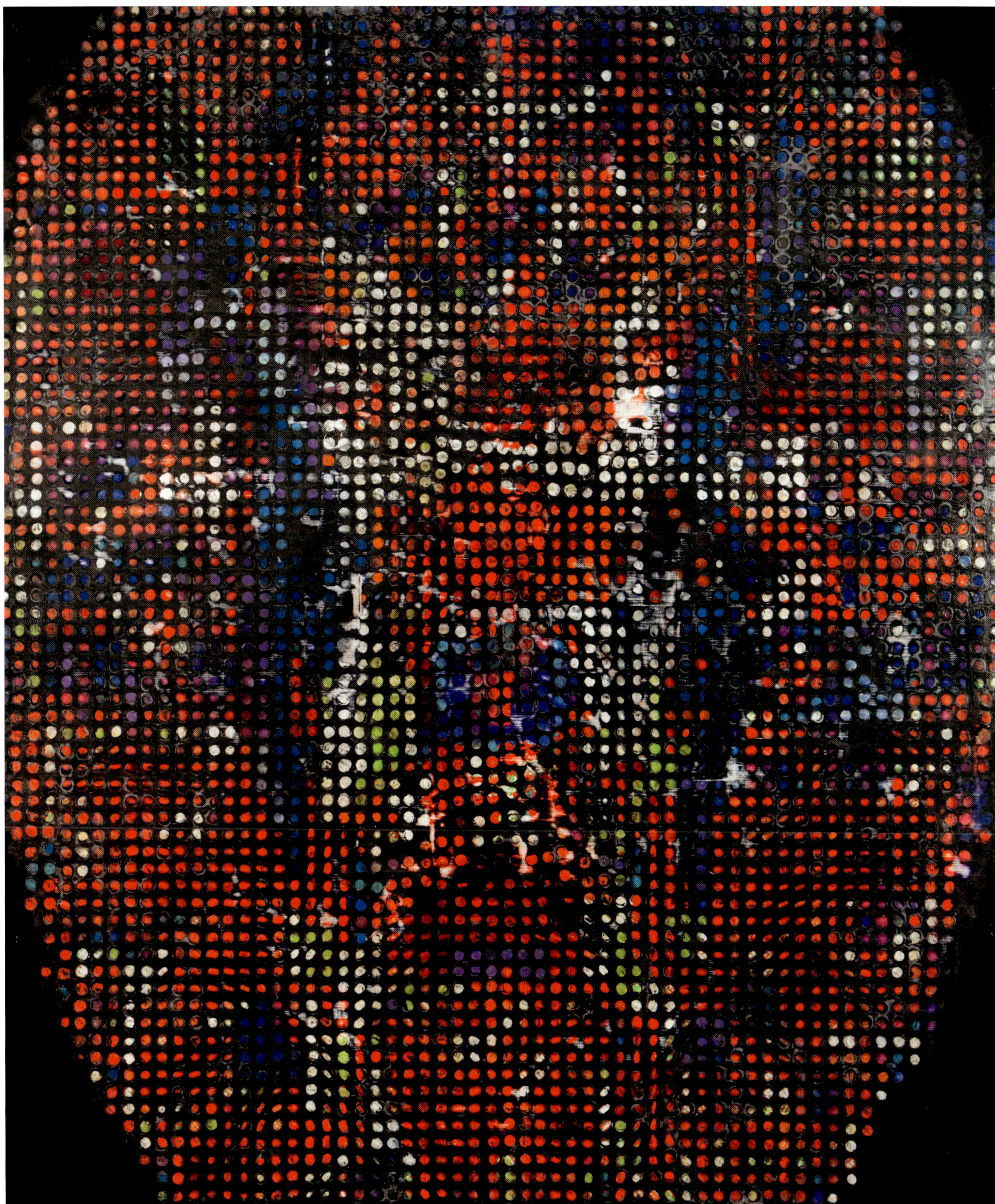

PLATE 4 **Christian Boltanski**, *Untitled (Reserve)*, 1989

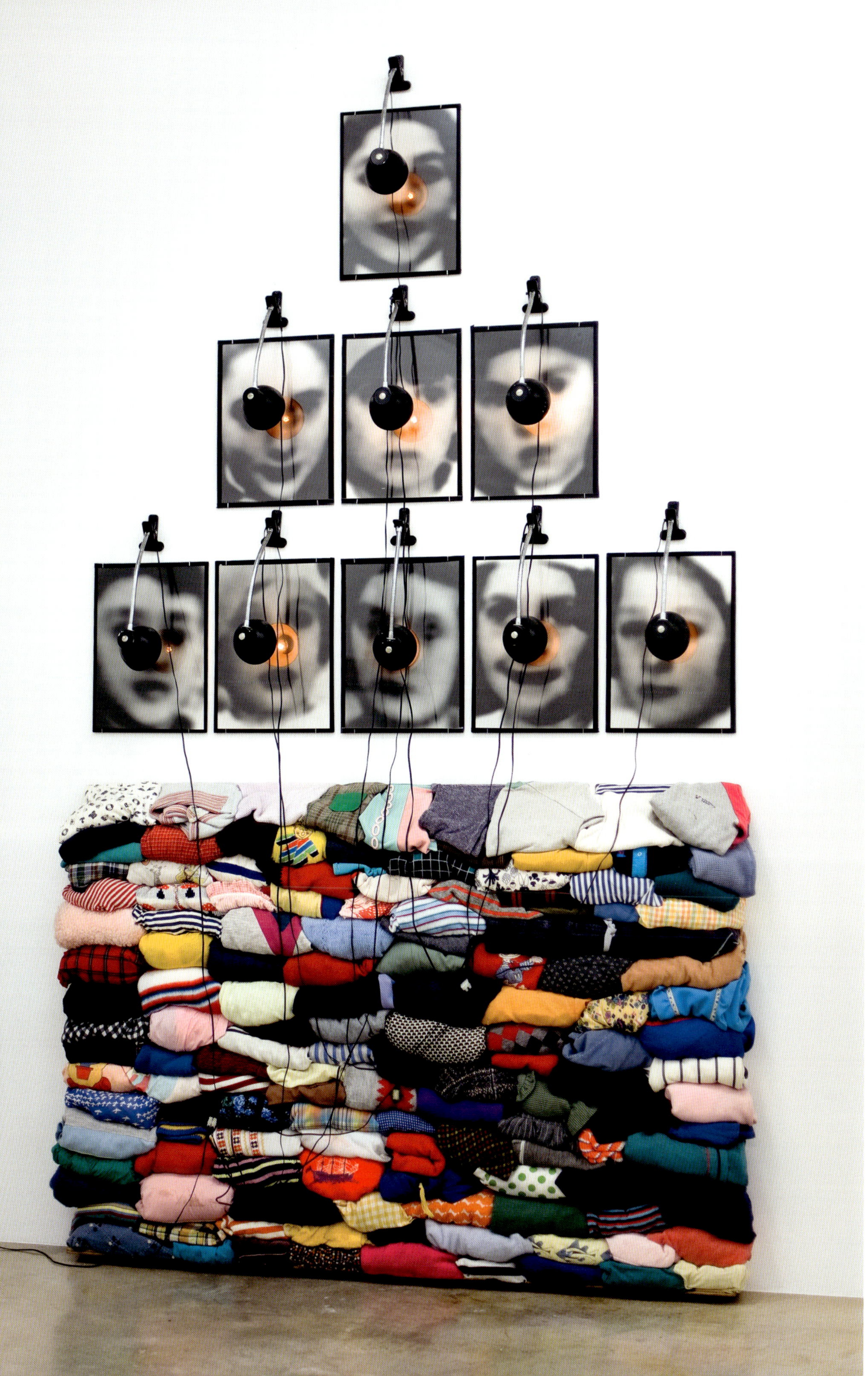

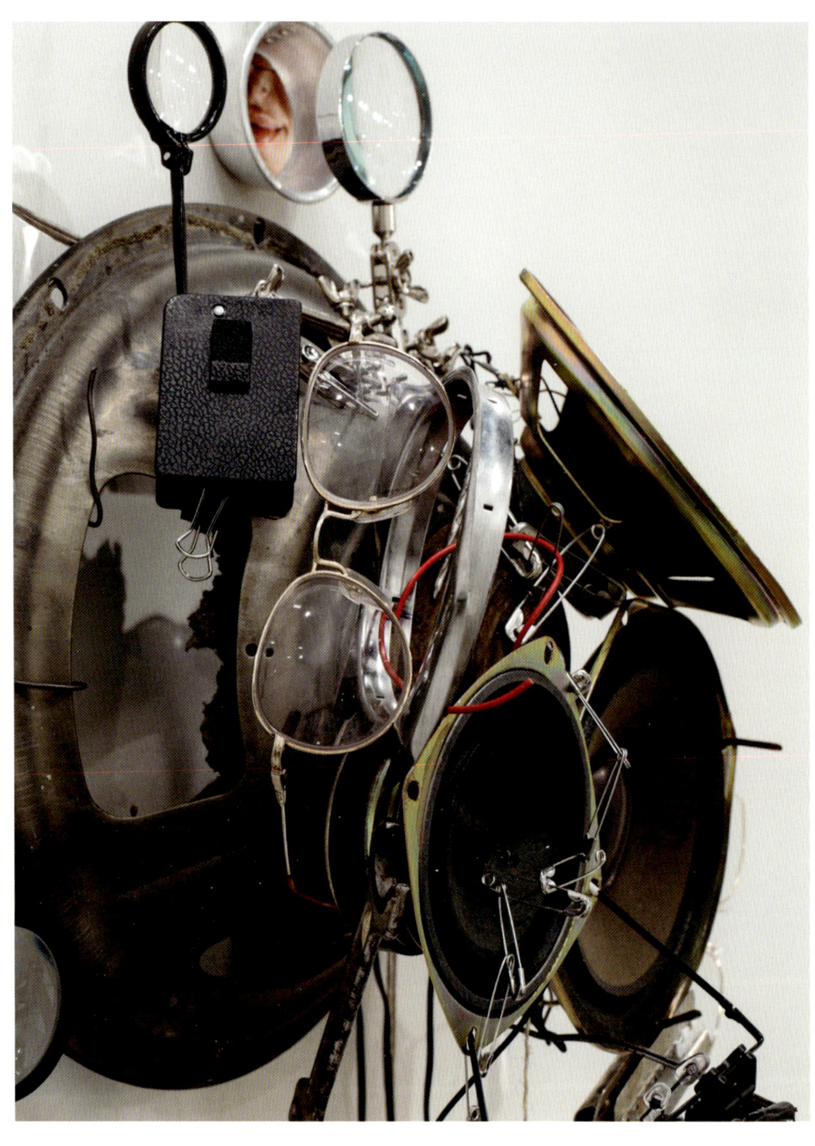

PLATE 5 **Janet Cardiff** and **George Bures Miller**, *Exquisite Corpse, enfant*, 2012

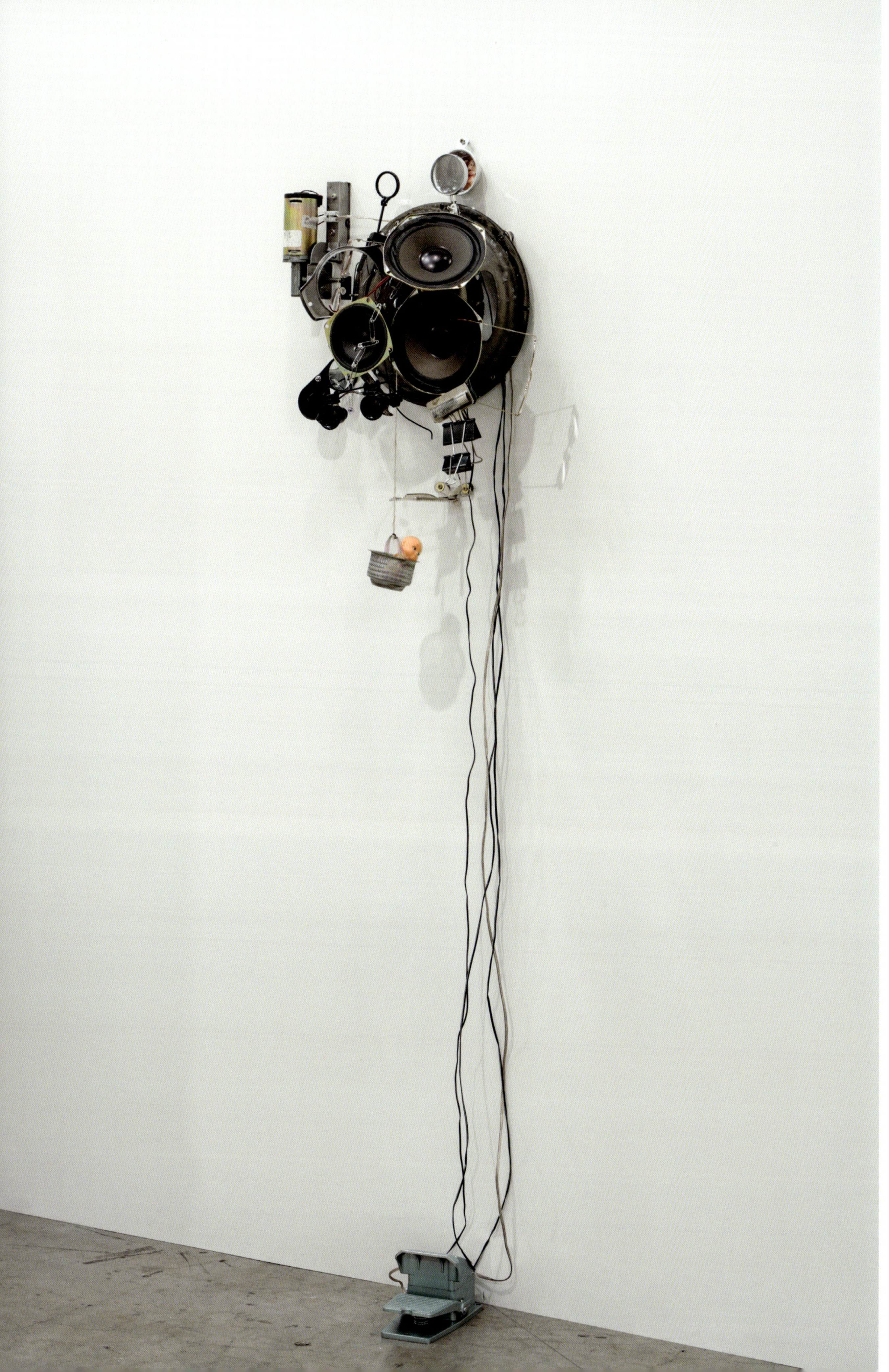

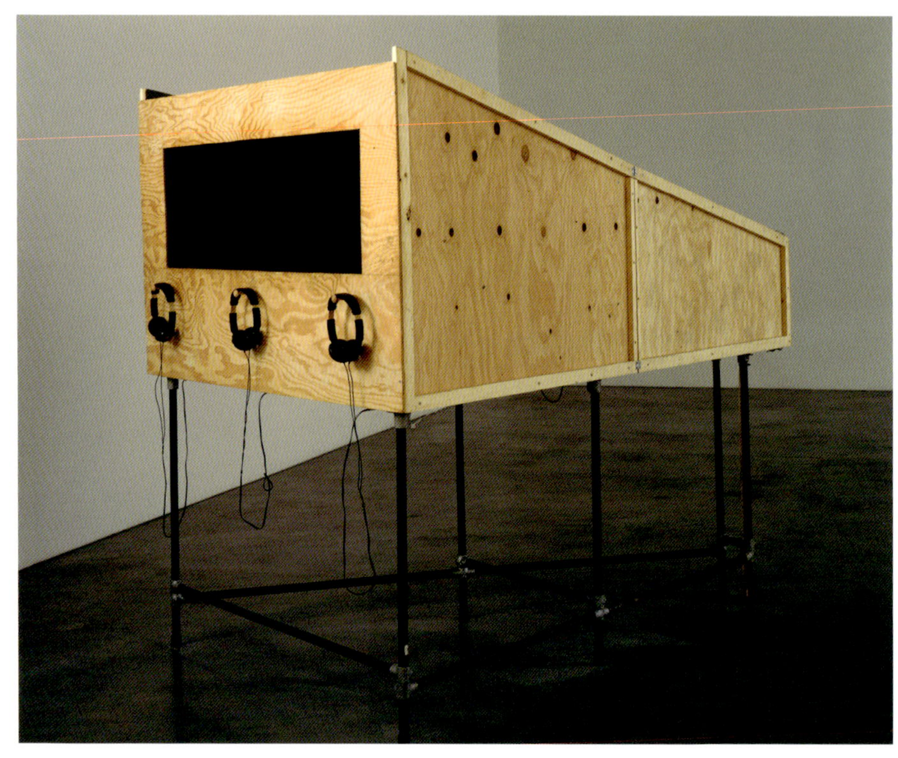

PLATE 6 **Janet Cardiff** and **George Bures Miller**, *The Muriel Lake Incident*, 1999

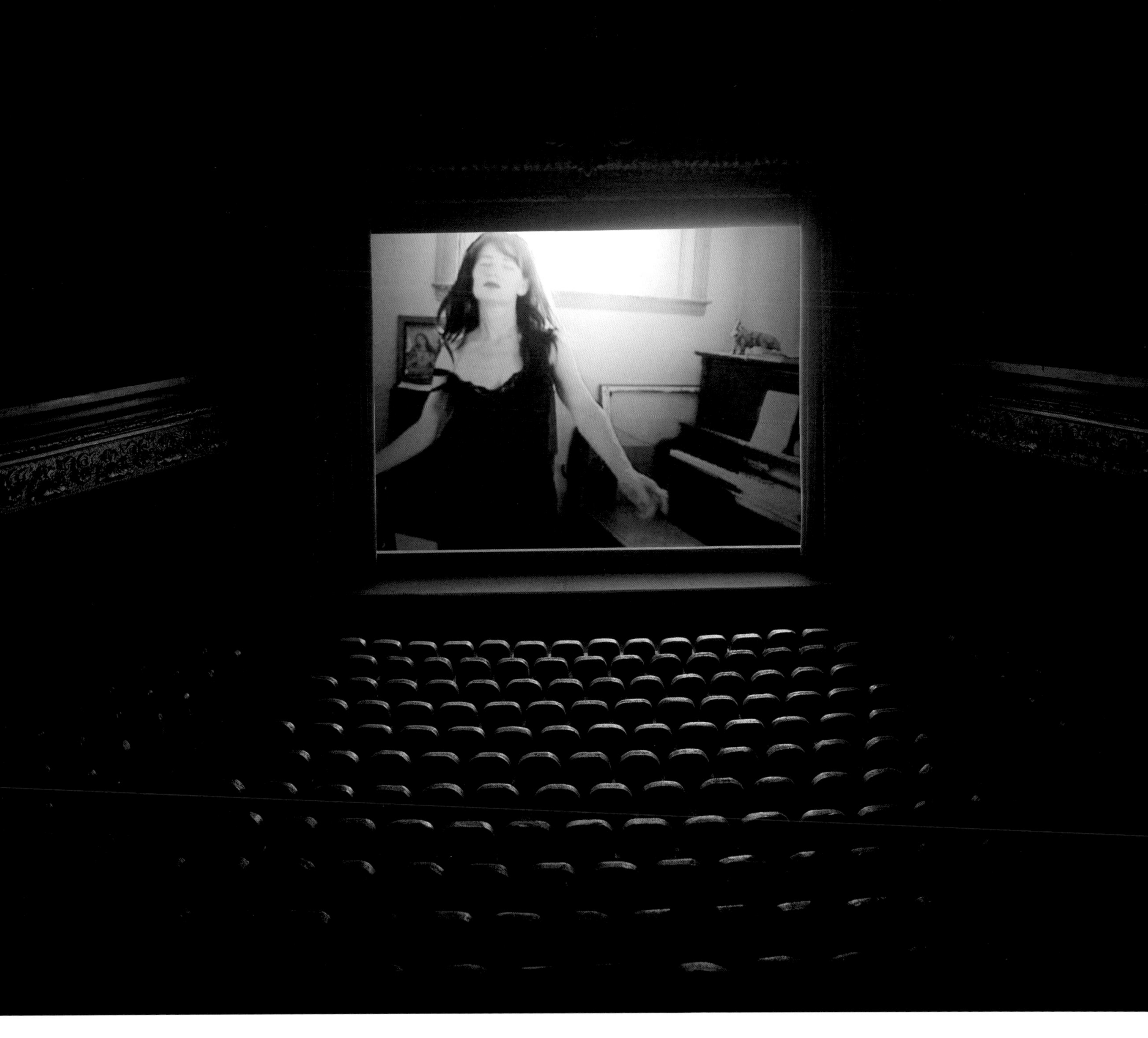

PLATE 7 **Adam Fuss**, *Home and the World*, 2010

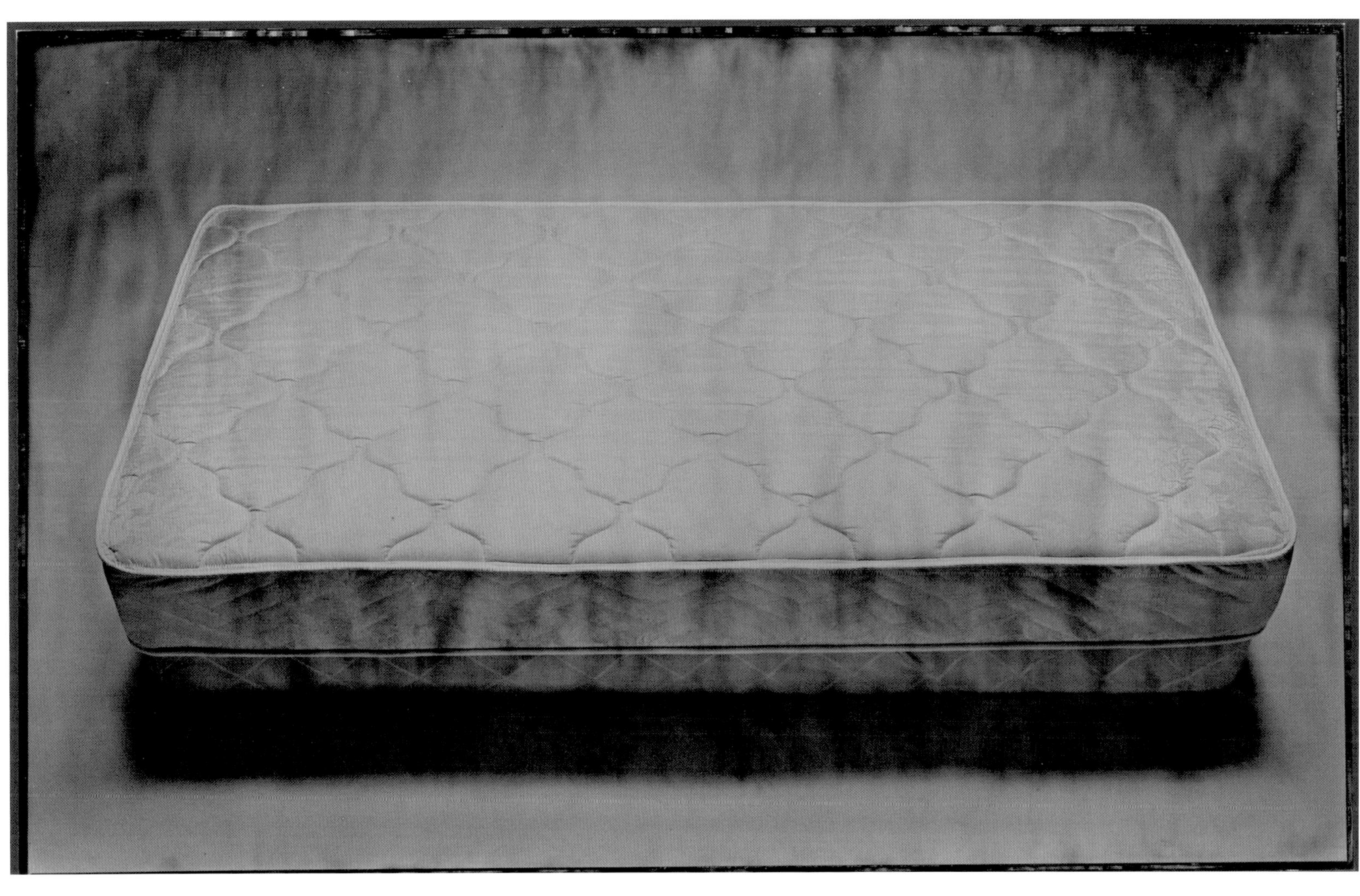

PLATE 8 **Adam Fuss**, *Medusa*, 2010

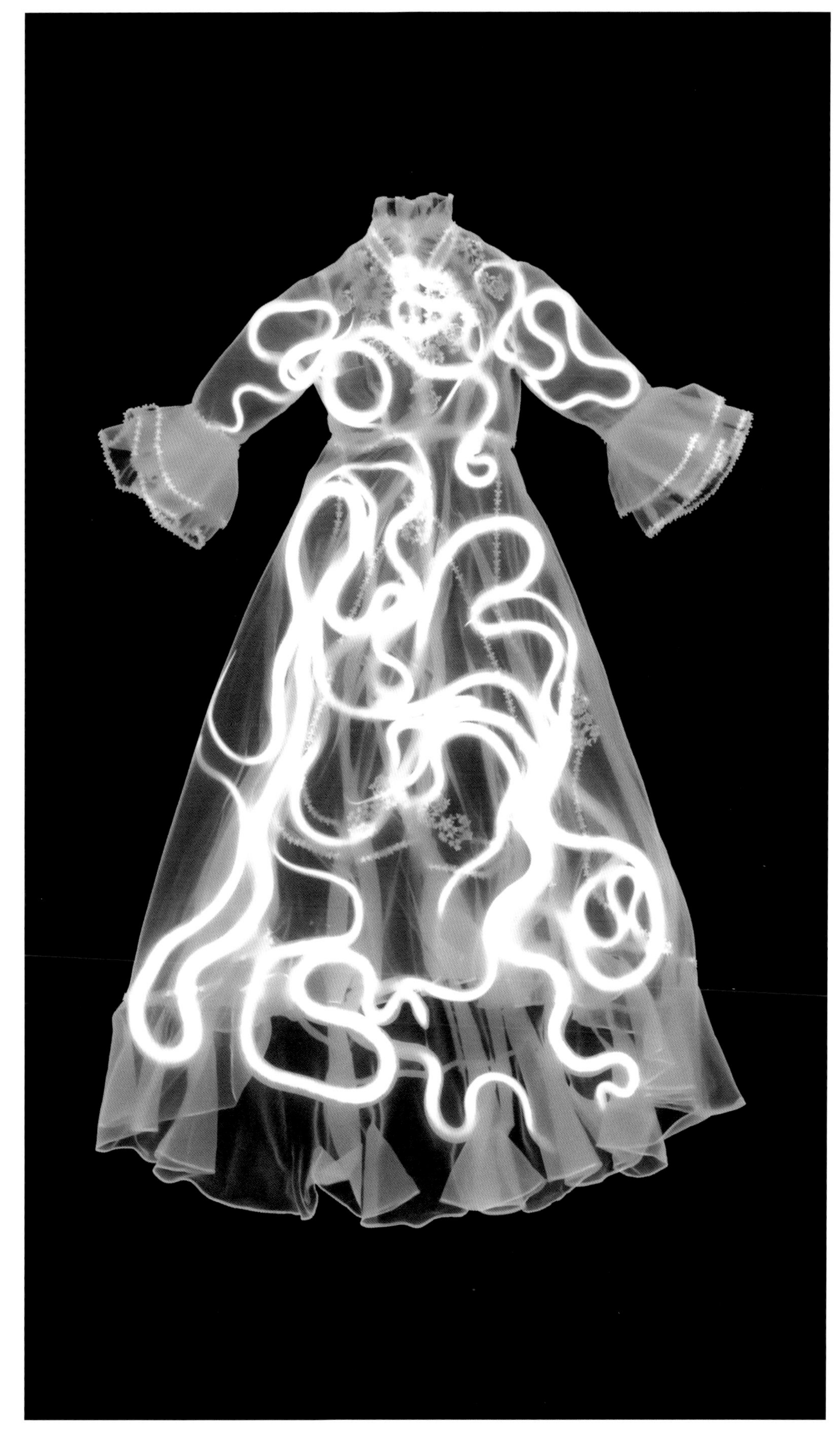

PLATE 9 **Adam Fuss**, *Untitled*, 2002

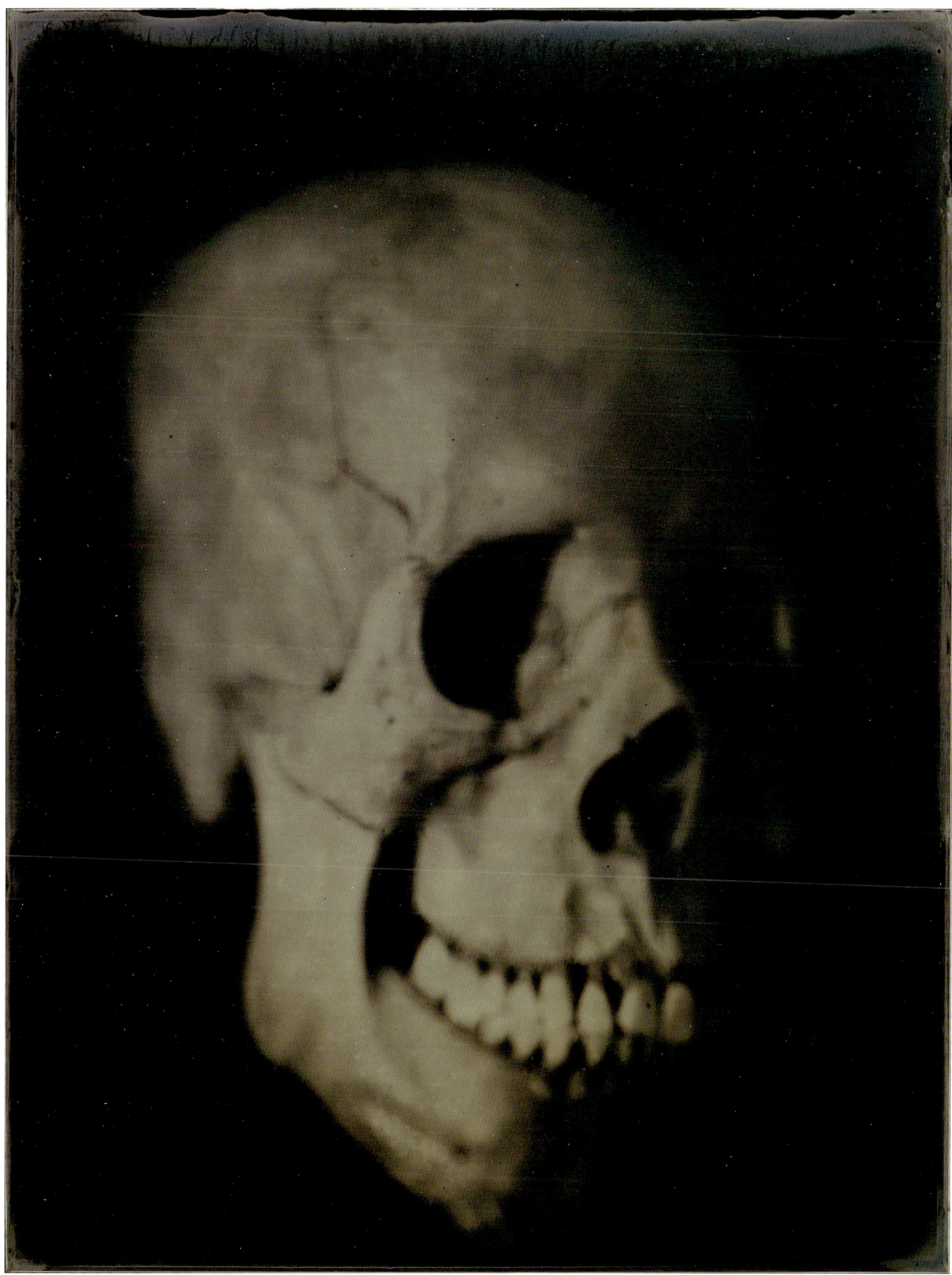

PLATE 10 **Adam Fuss**, *Untitled*, 2006

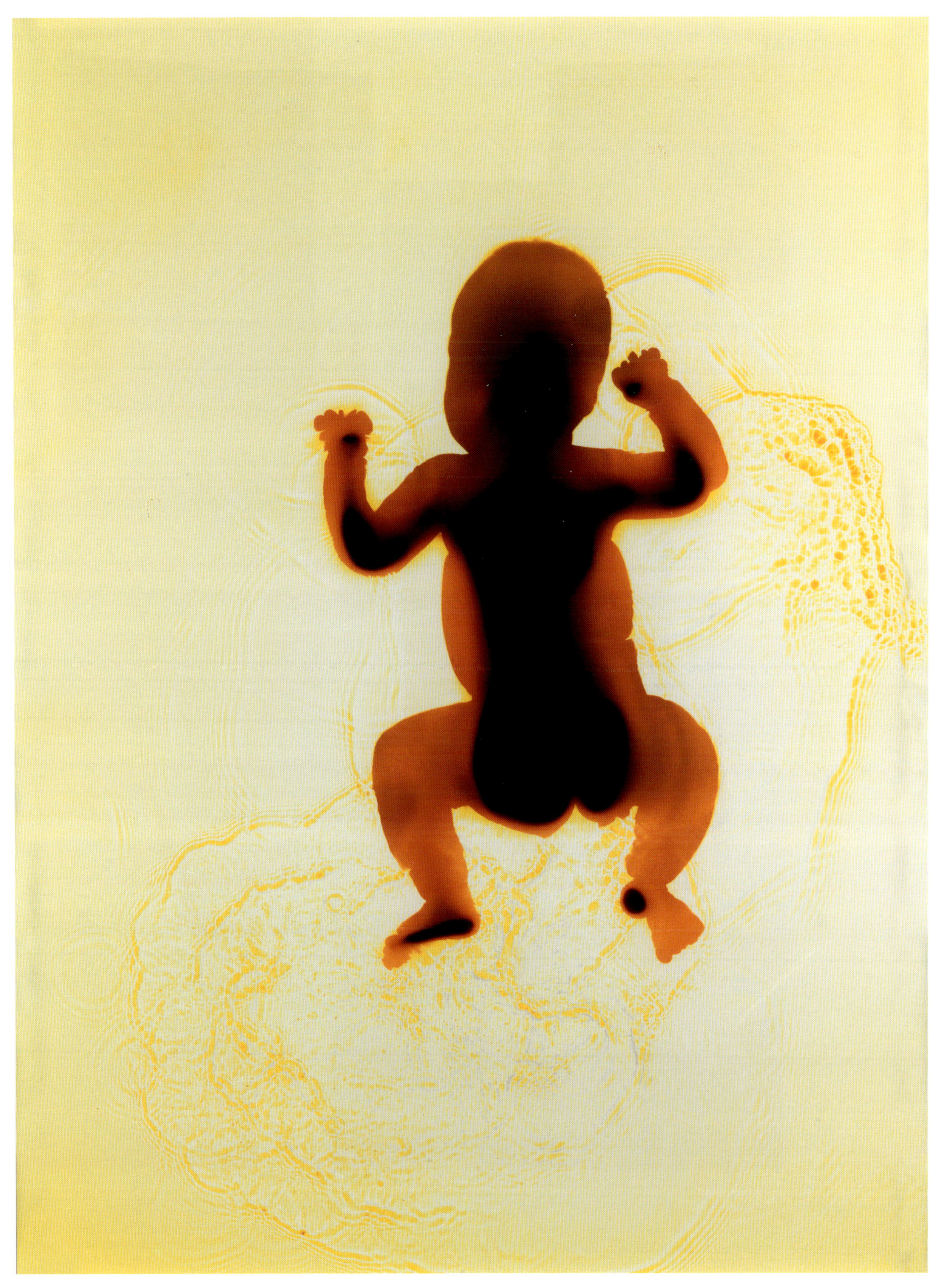

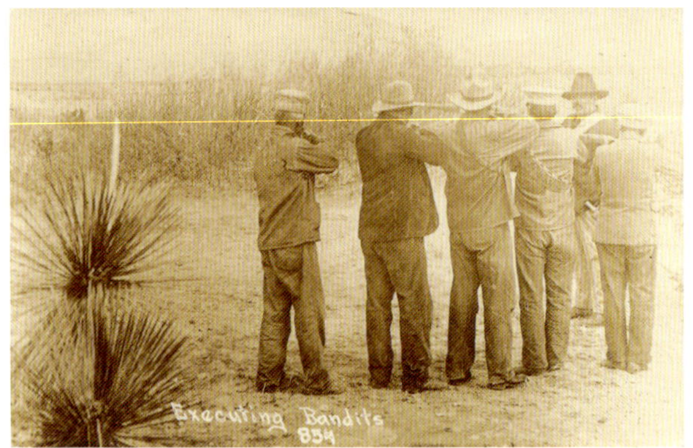

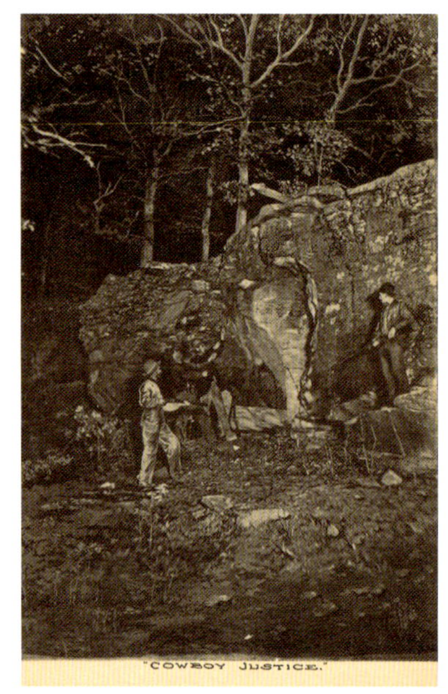

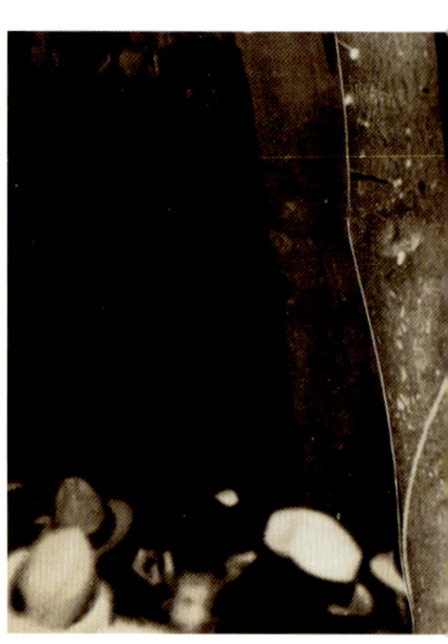

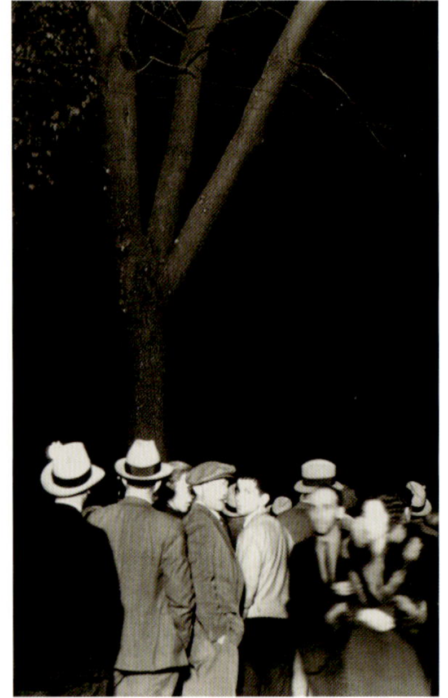

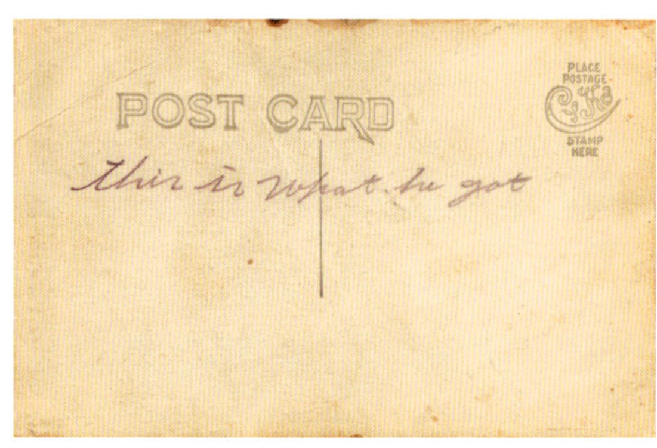

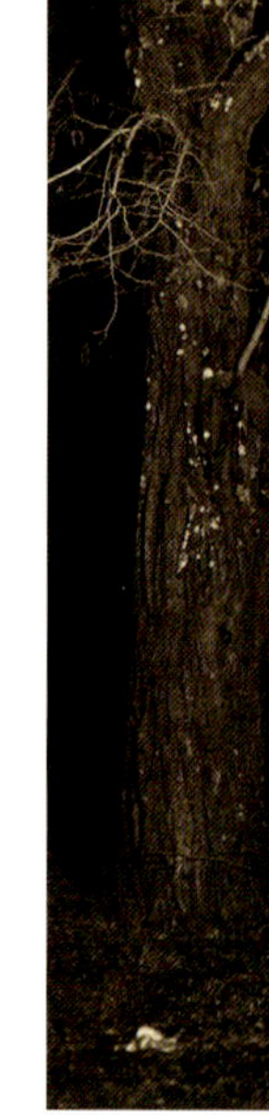

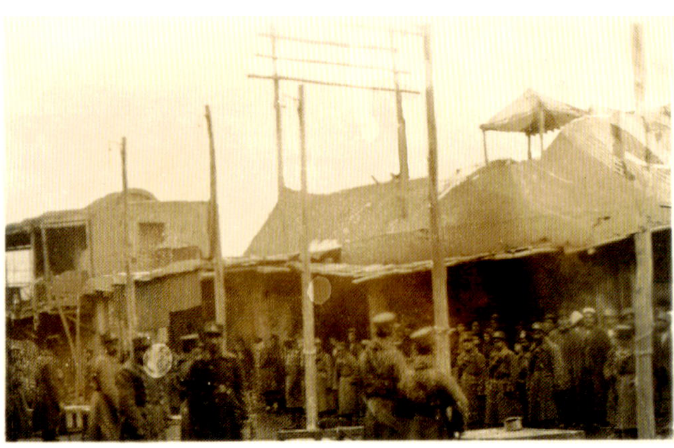

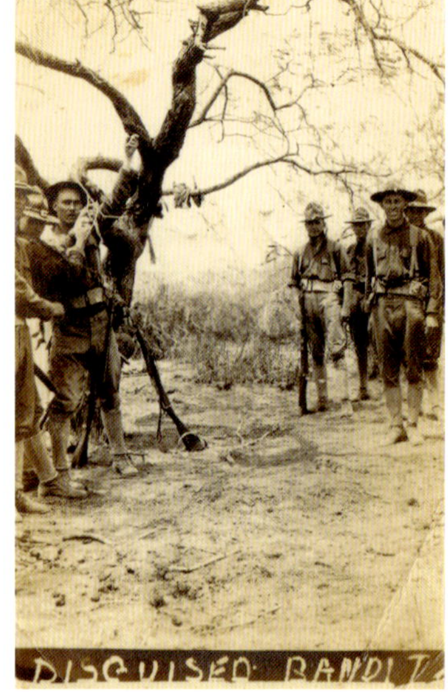

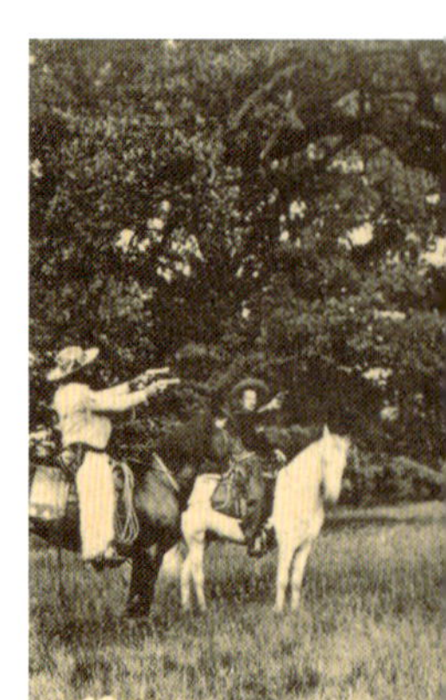

PLATE 11 **Ken Gonzales-Day**, *Erased Lynchings*, 2004

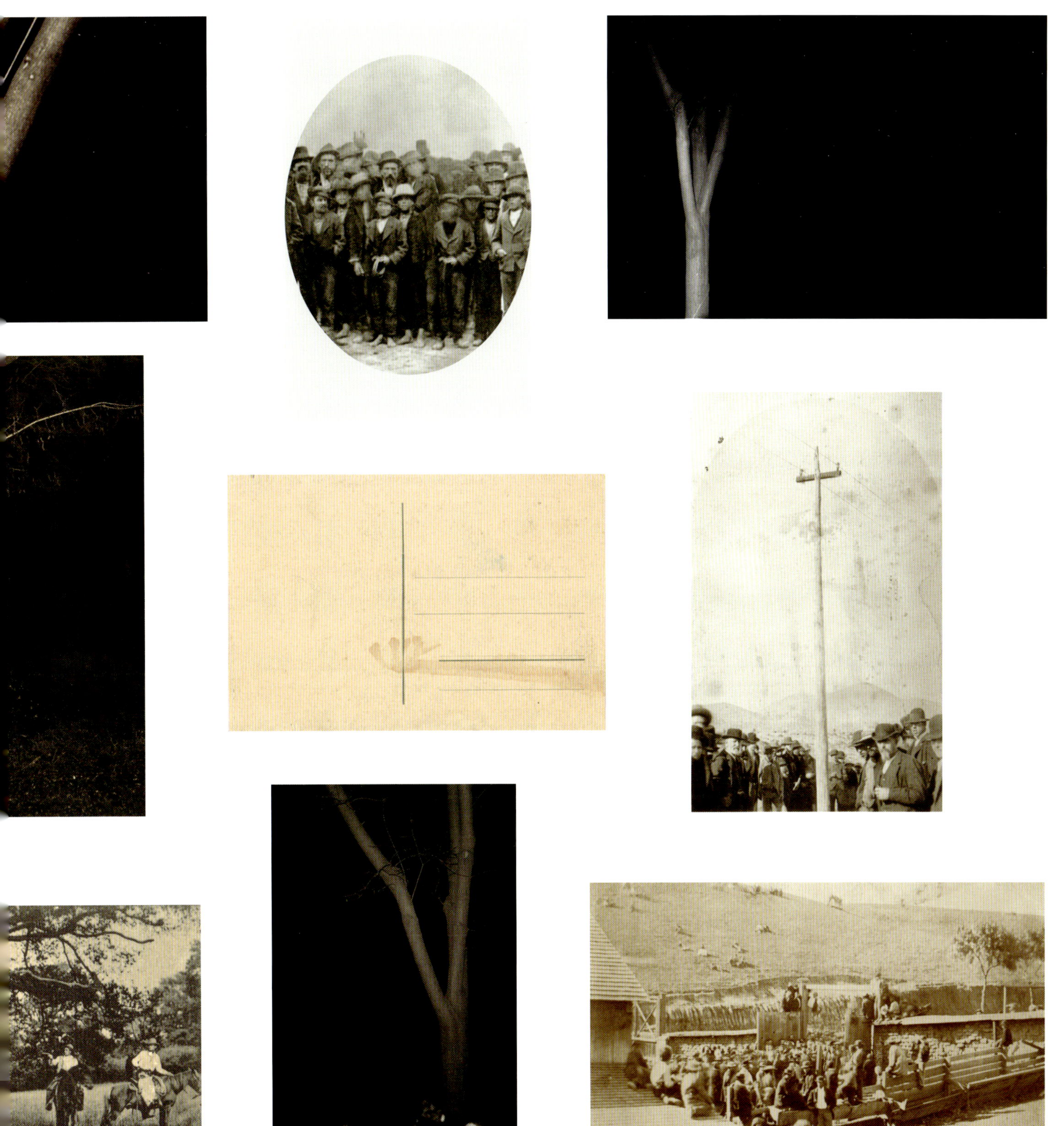

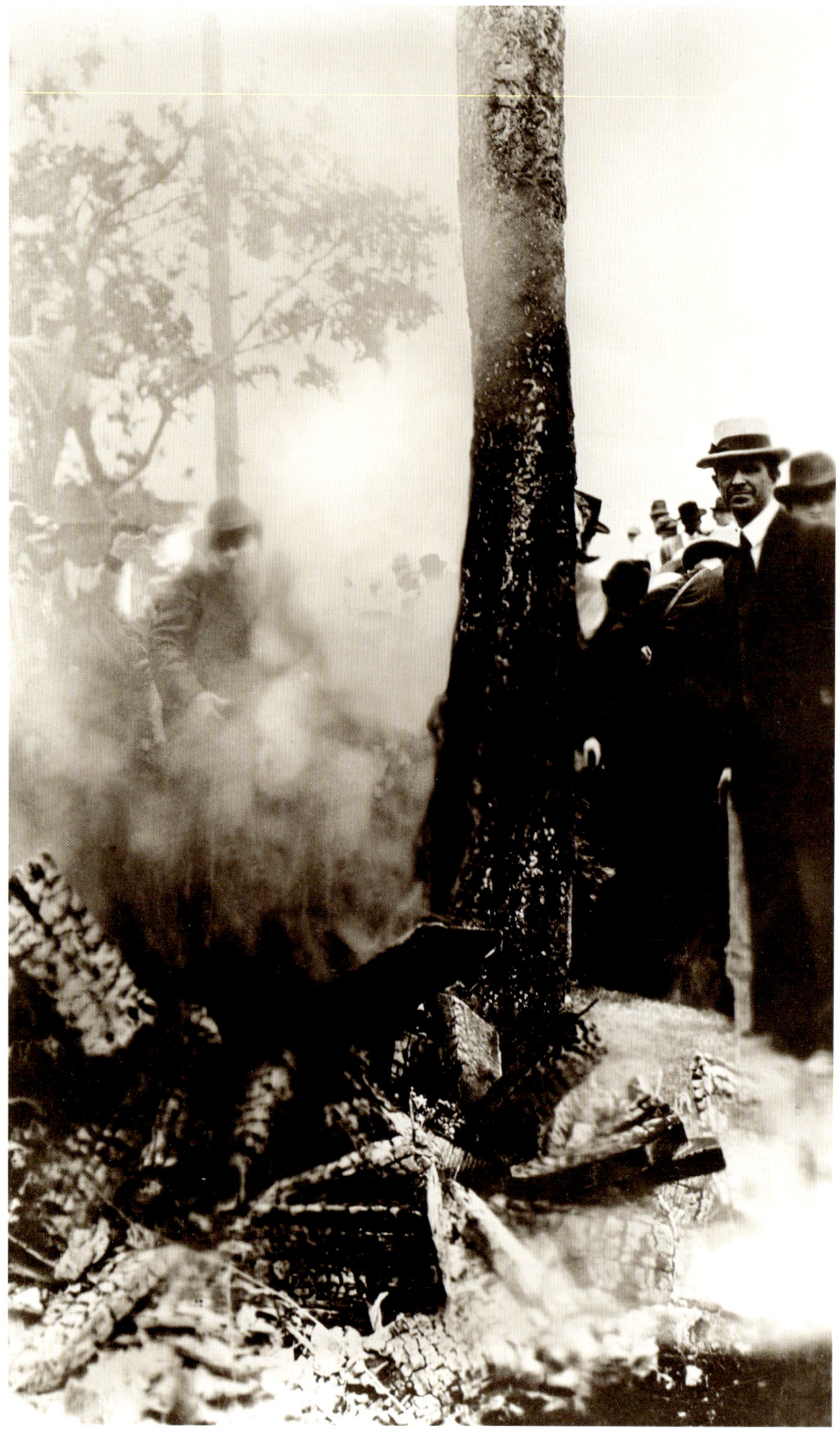

PLATE 12 **Ken Gonzales-Day**, *Waco, TX*, 2013

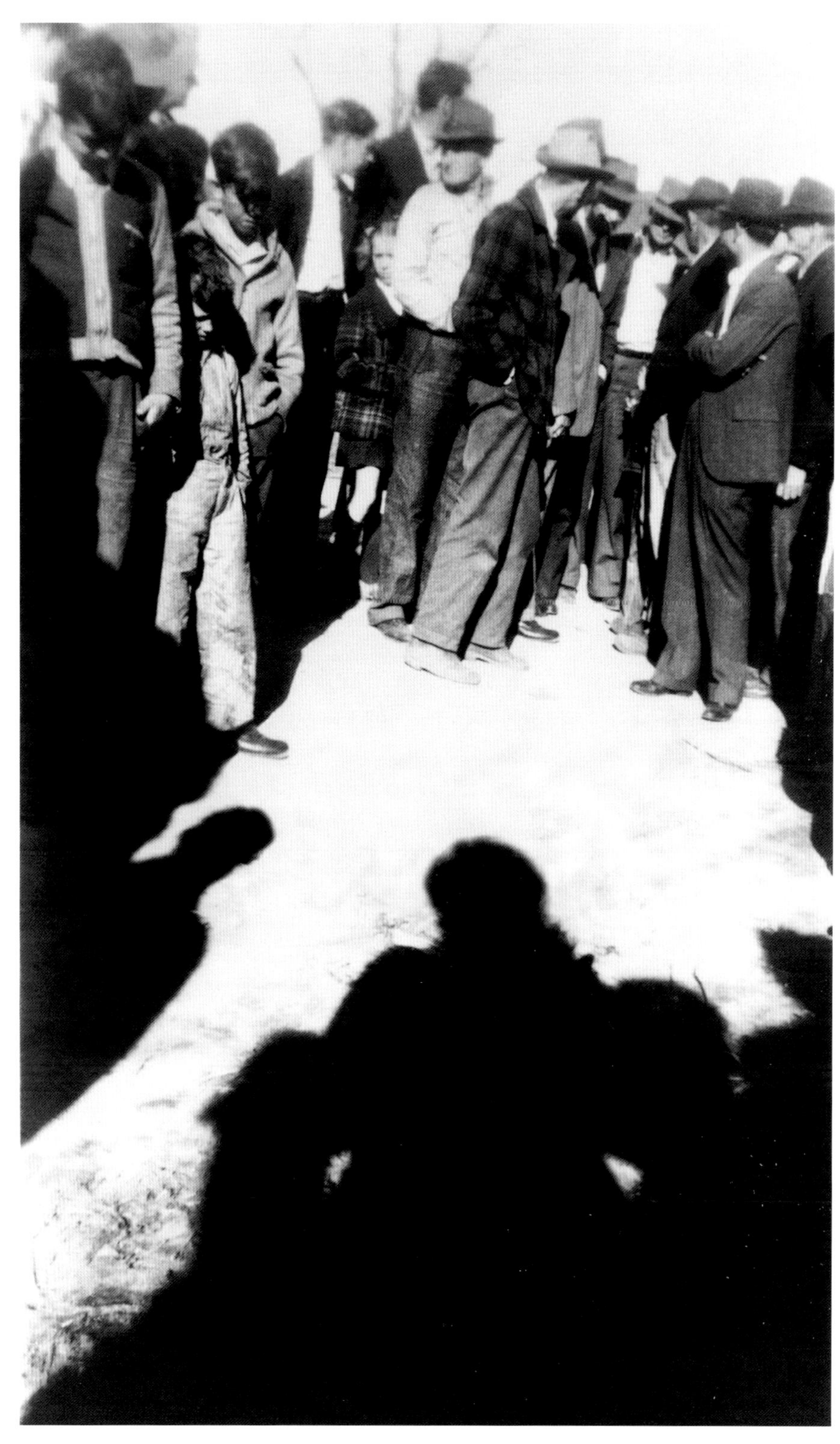

PLATE 13 **Ken Gonzales-Day**, *Sikeston, MO*, 2013

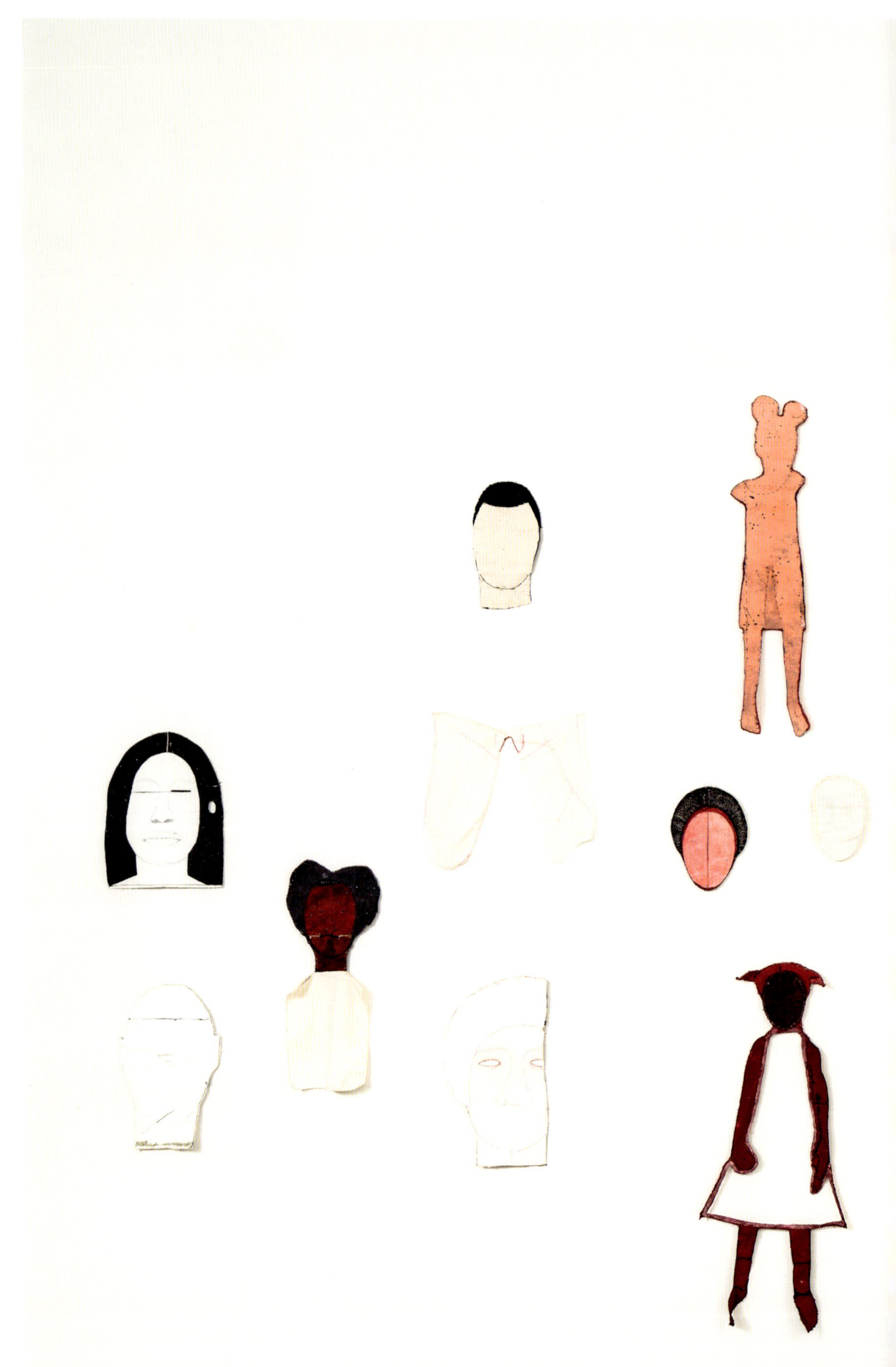

PLATE 14 **Alicia Henry**, *Untitled (Brown, Red, White, and Blue)*, 2012–15

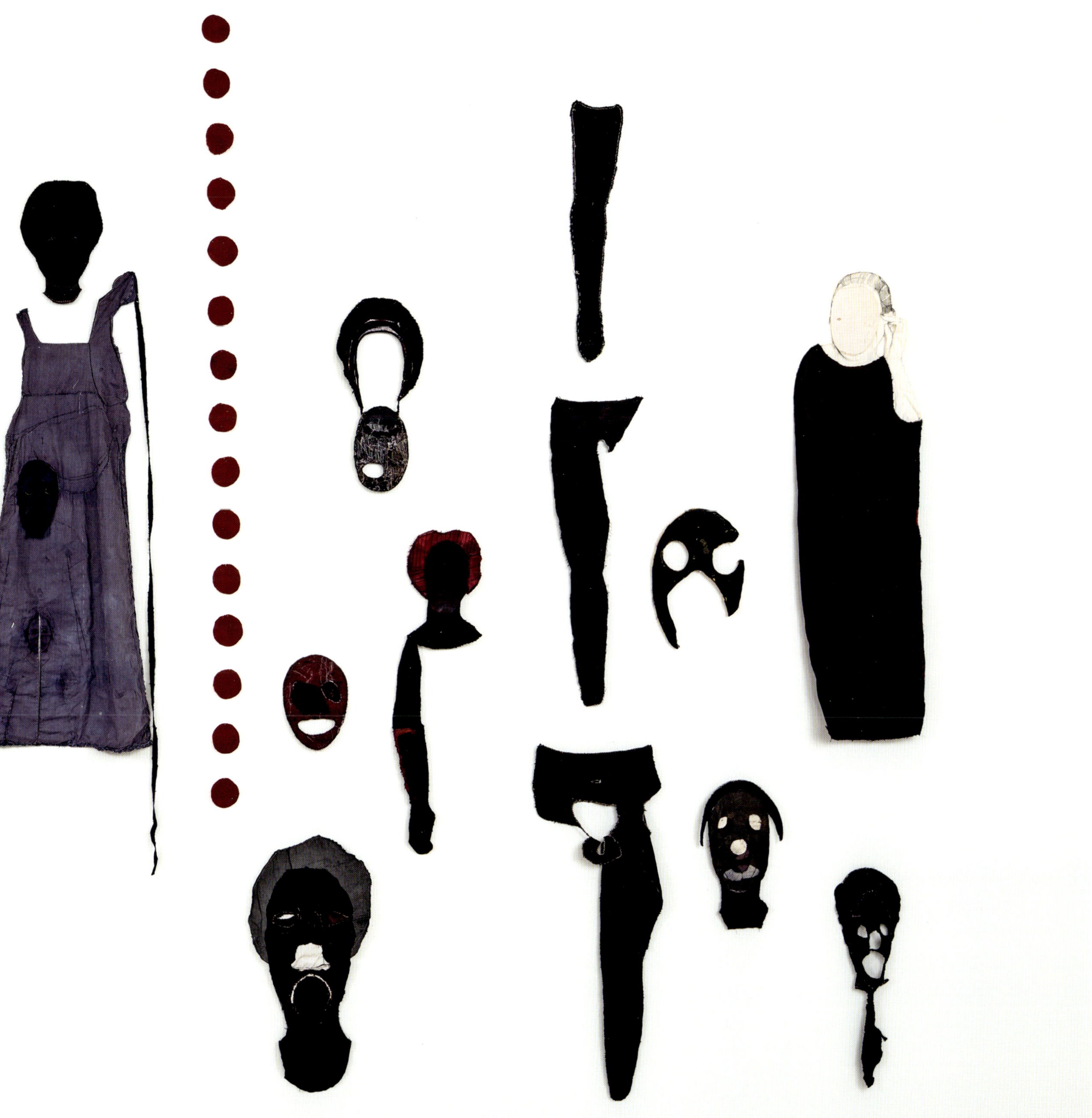

PLATE 15 **Damien Hirst**, *The Unbearable Lightness of Being*, 2003

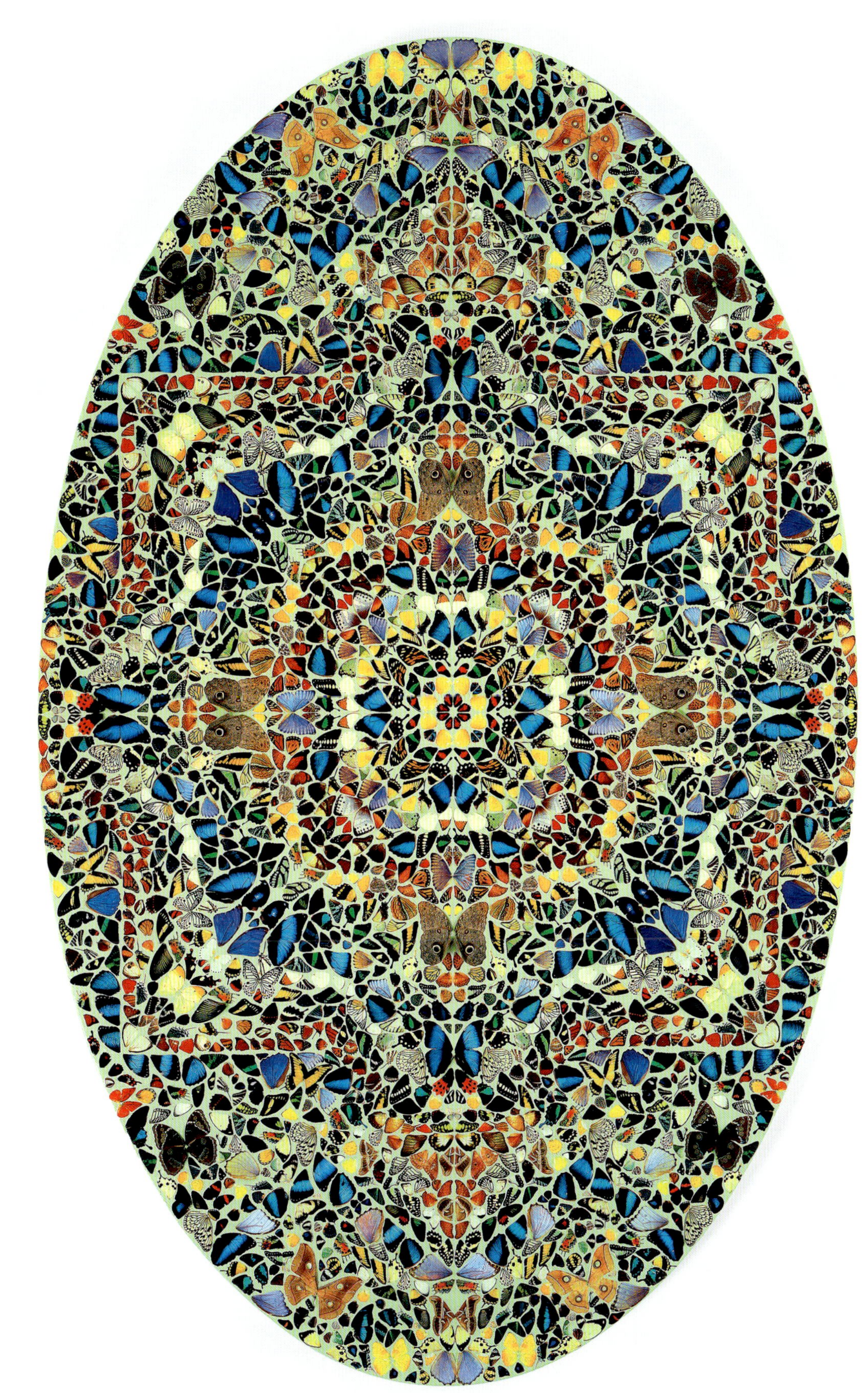

PLATE 16 **Shirazeh Houshiary**, *Ode*, 2013

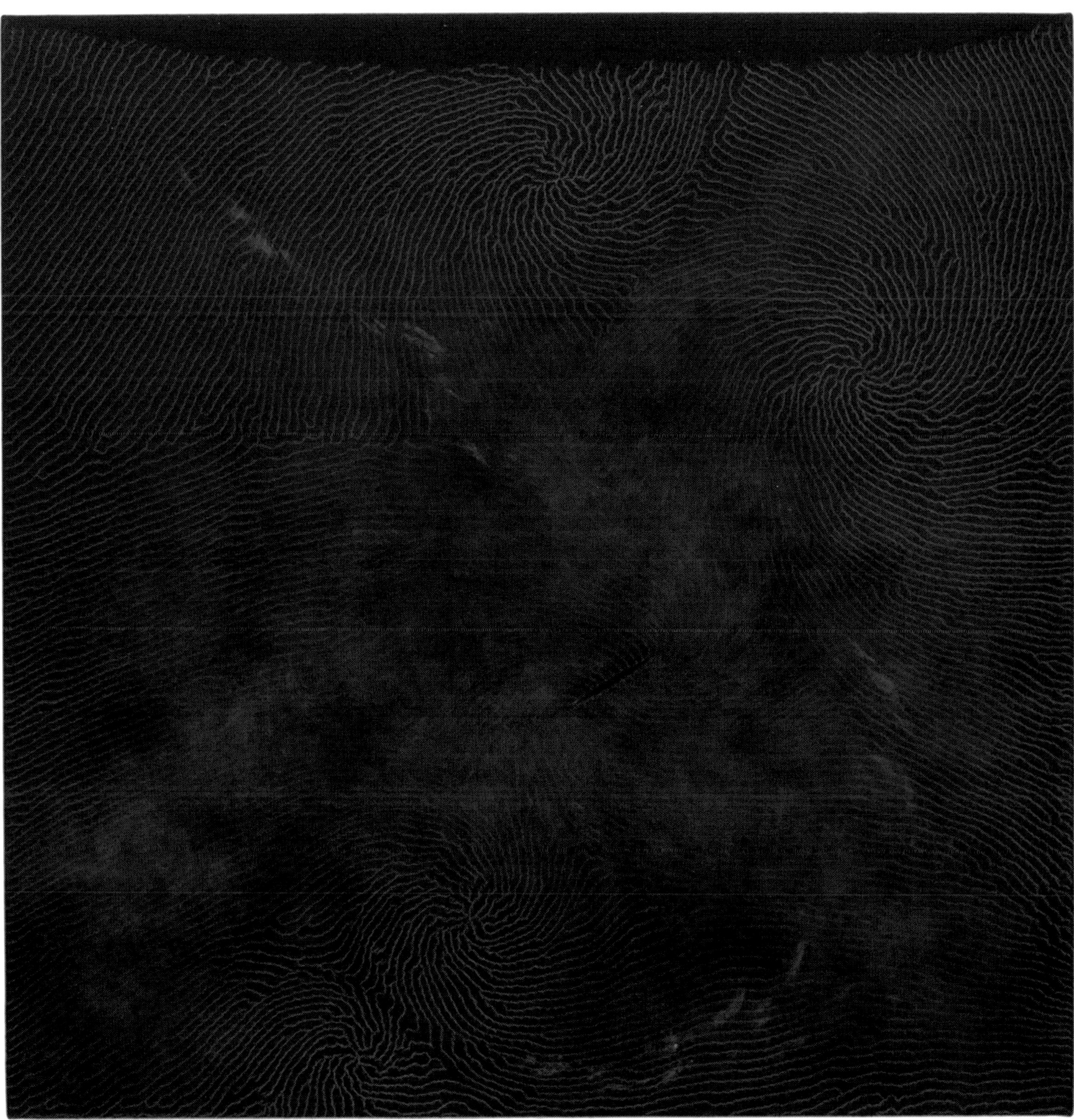

PLATE 17 **Anish Kapoor**, *Mother as a Mountain*, 1985

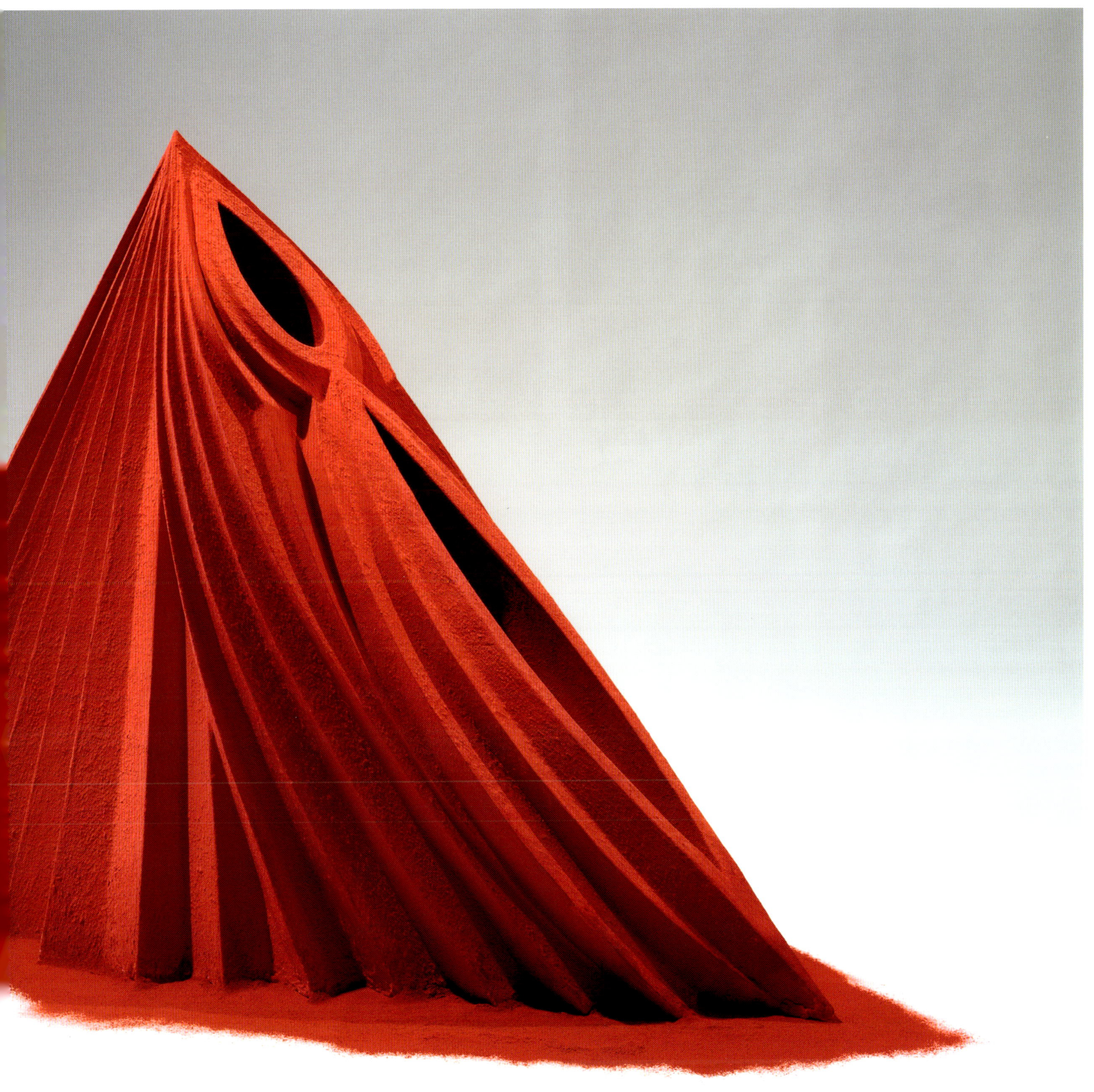

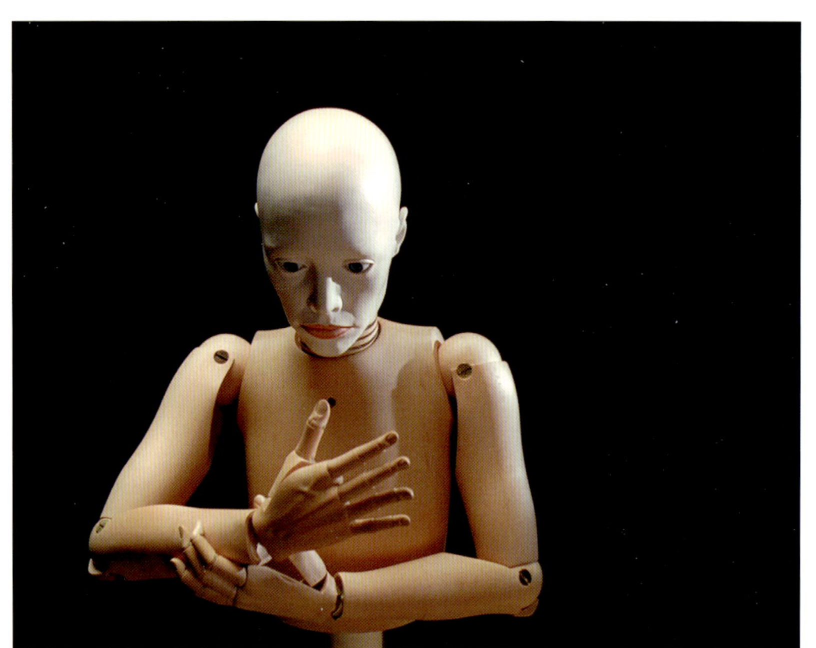

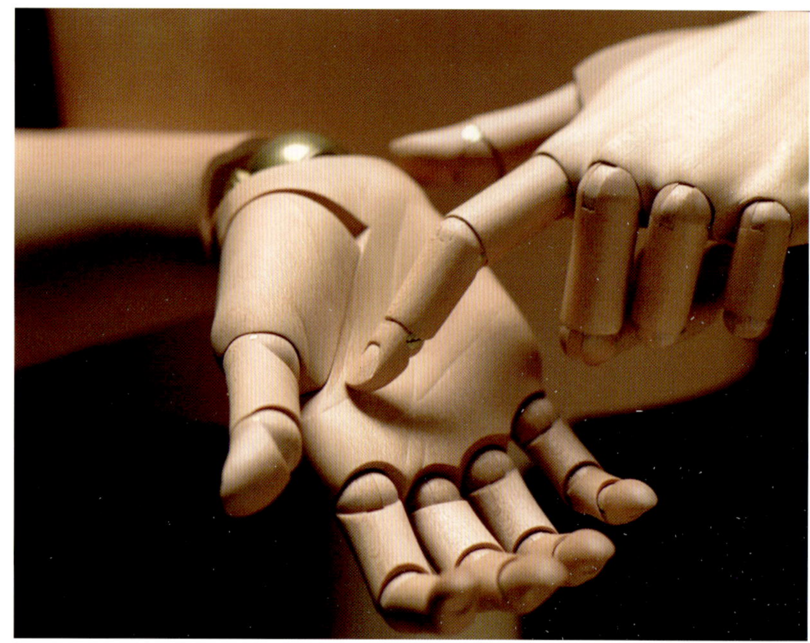

PLATE 18 **Elizabeth King** and **Richard Kizu-Blair**, *What Happened*, 1991
(remastered for high-definition video, 2008)

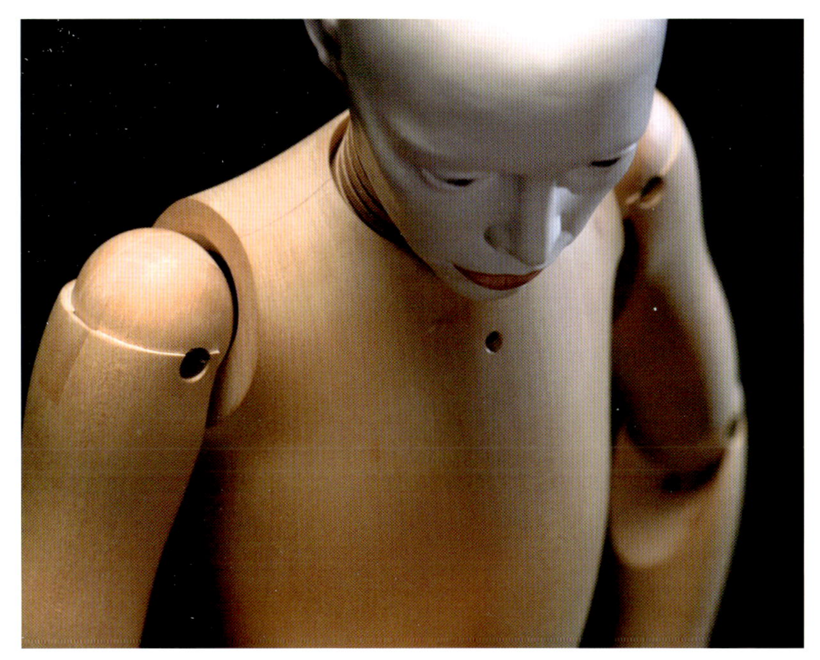
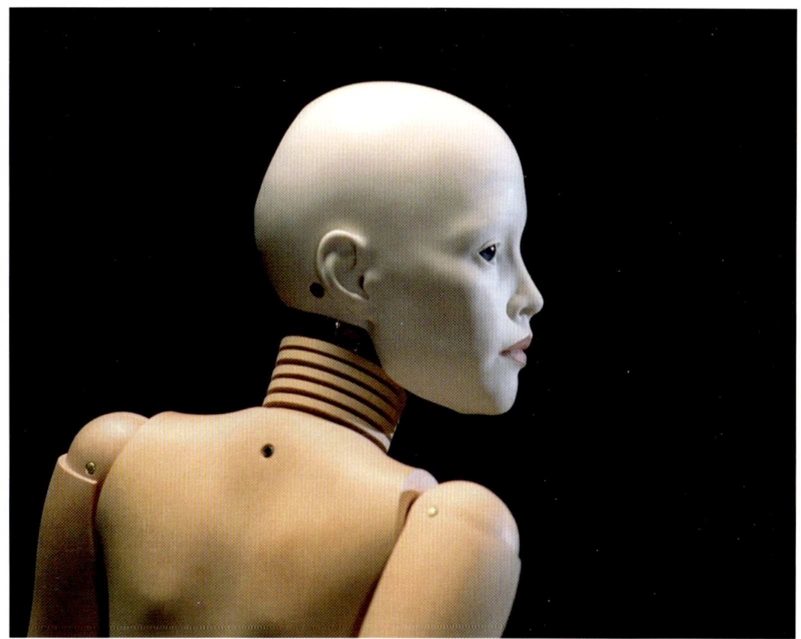

PLATE 19 **Elizabeth King**, *Pupil*, 1987–90

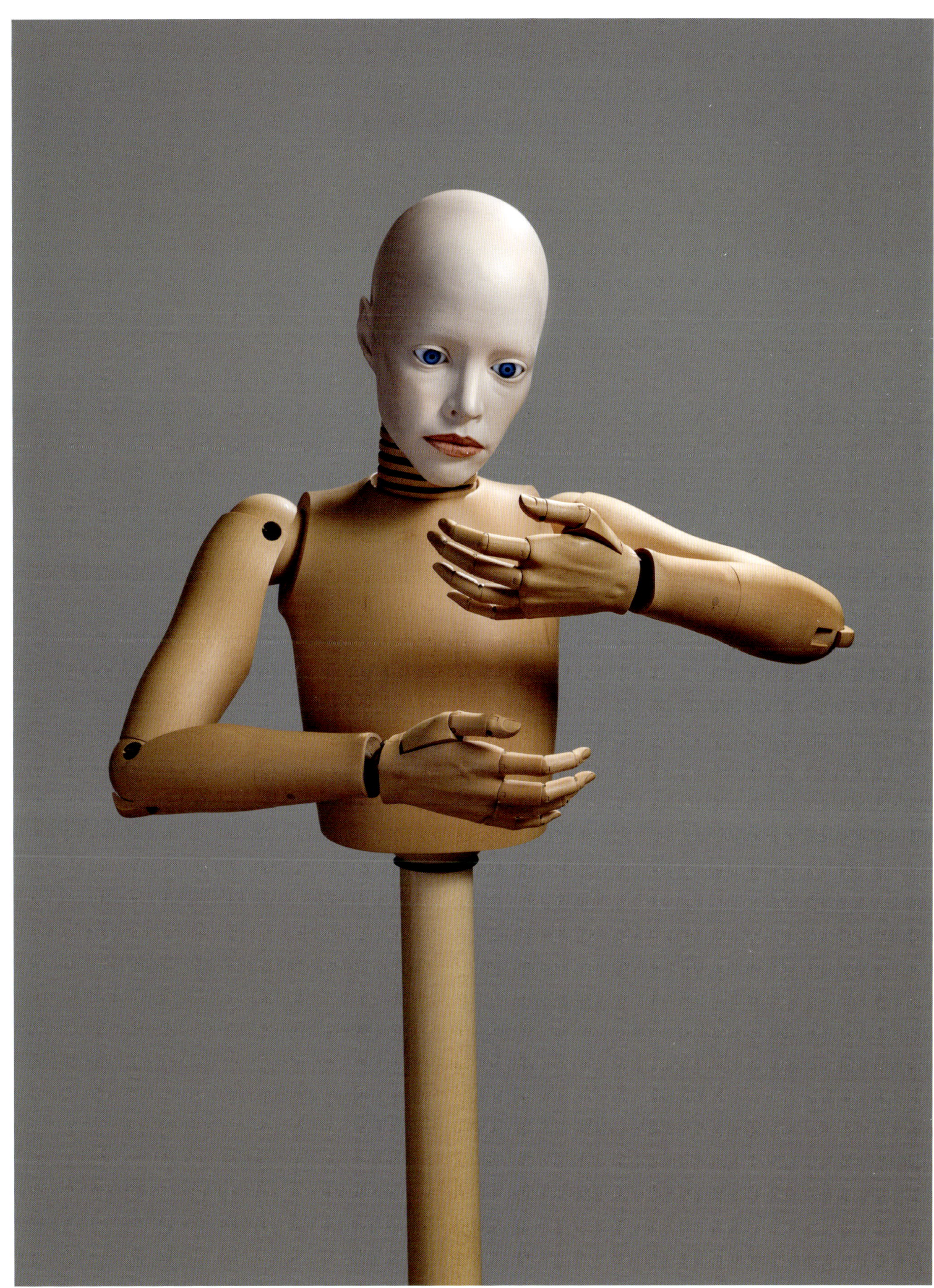

PLATE 20 **Deborah Luster**, *LSP143*, 1999

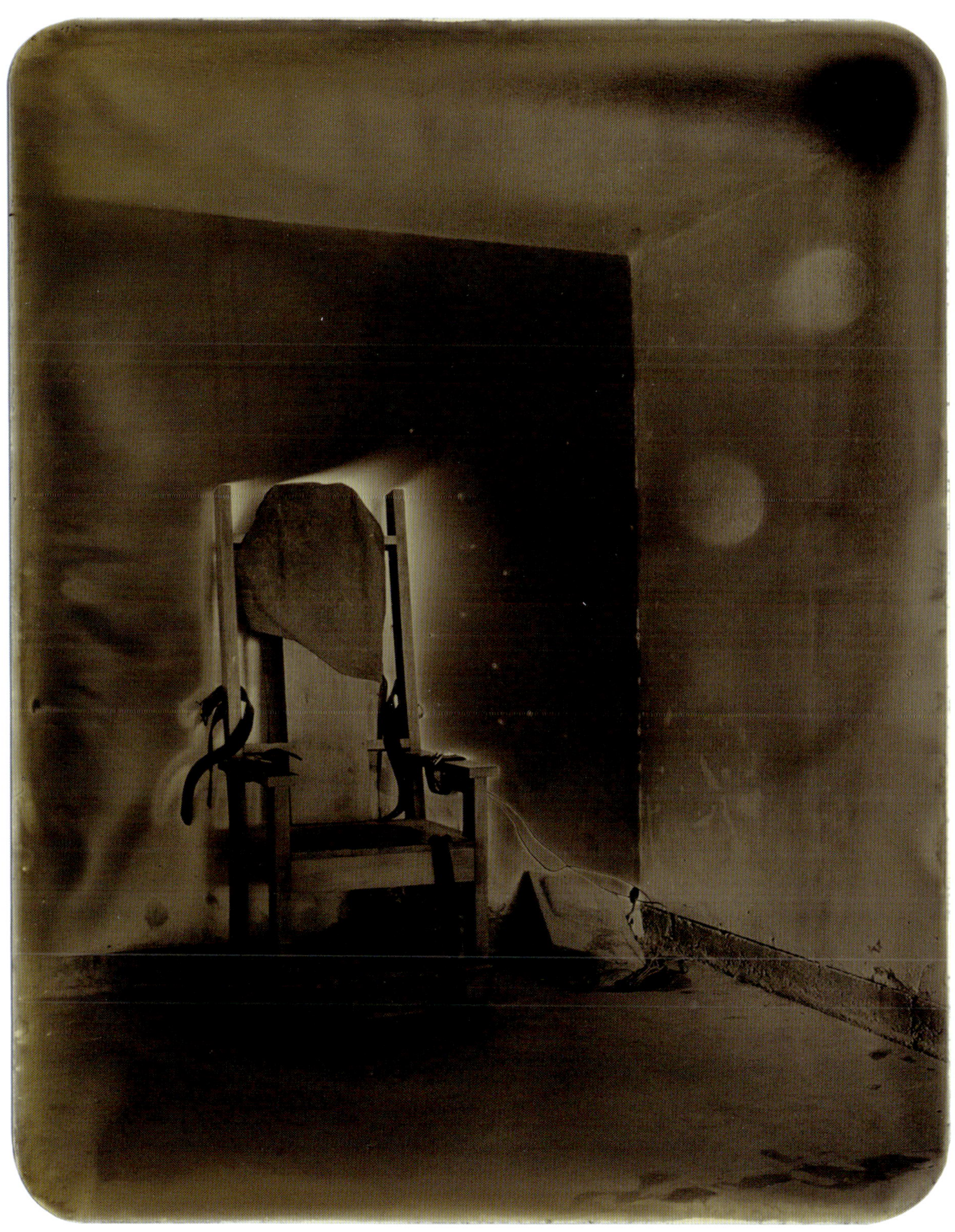

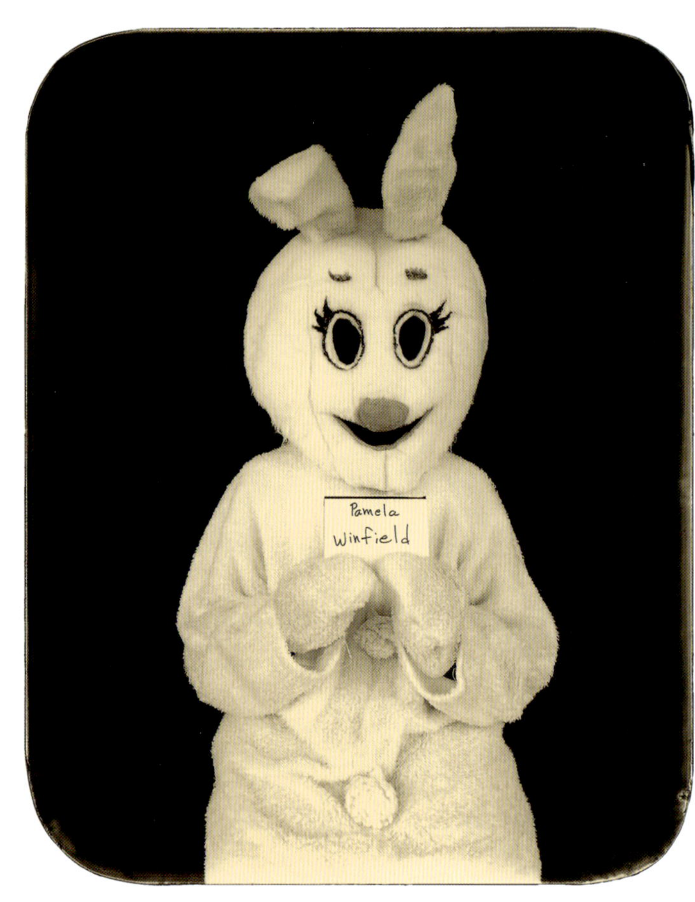

Deborah Luster

PLATE 21, TOP LEFT *LCIW91*, 2000

PLATE 22, TOP CENTER *LCIW82*, 2000

PLATE 23, TOP RIGHT *LCIW81*, 2000

PLATE 24, BOTTOM CENTER *LCIW85*, 2000

PLATE 25, BOTTOM RIGHT *LCIW83*, 1999

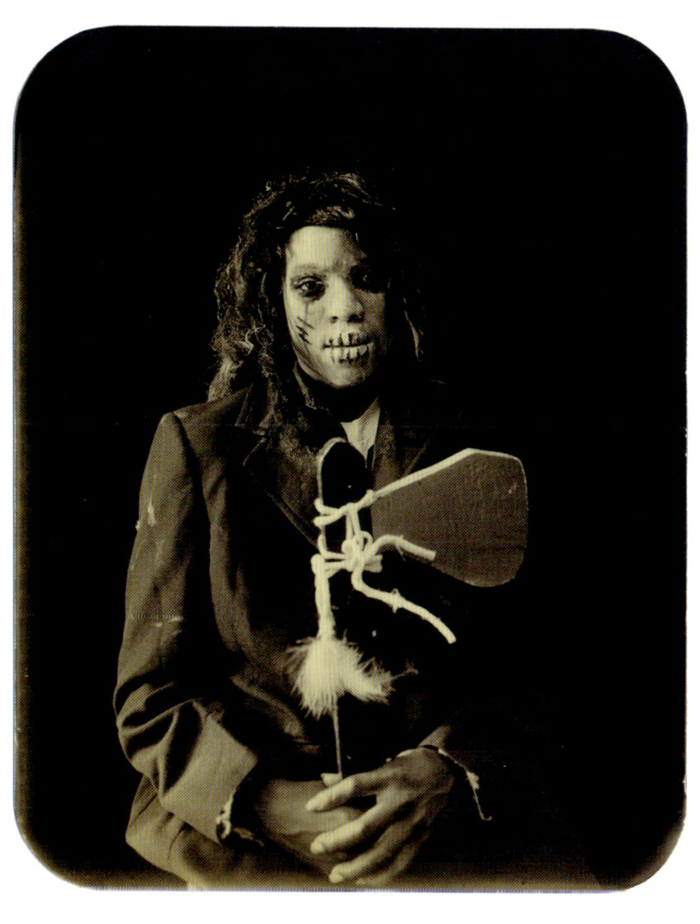
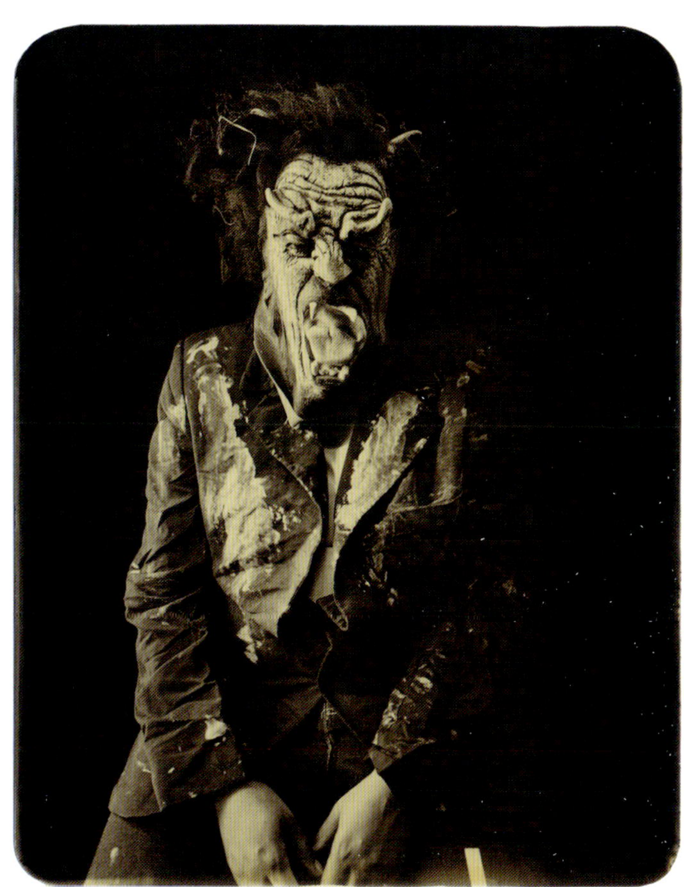
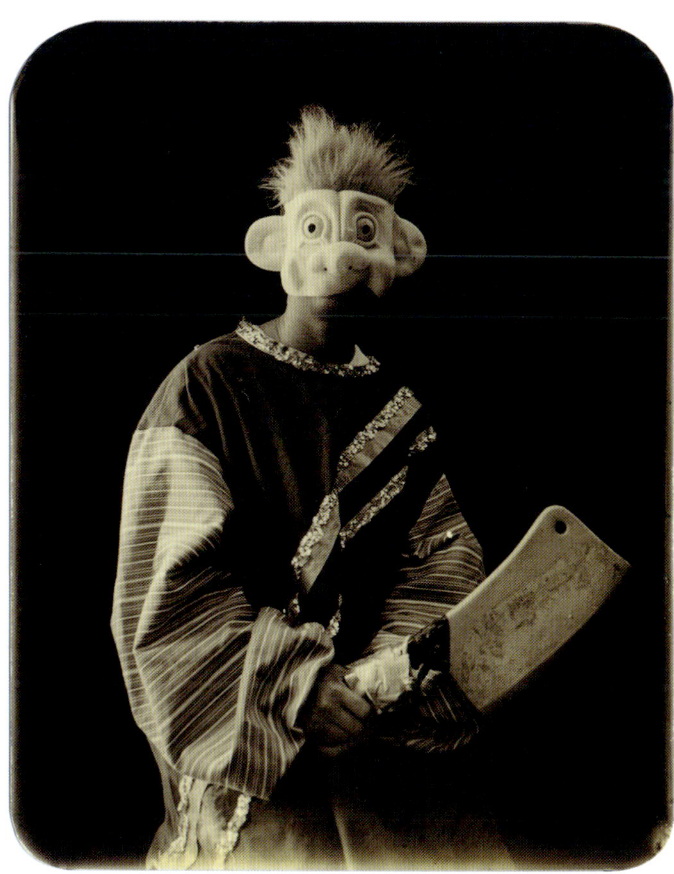
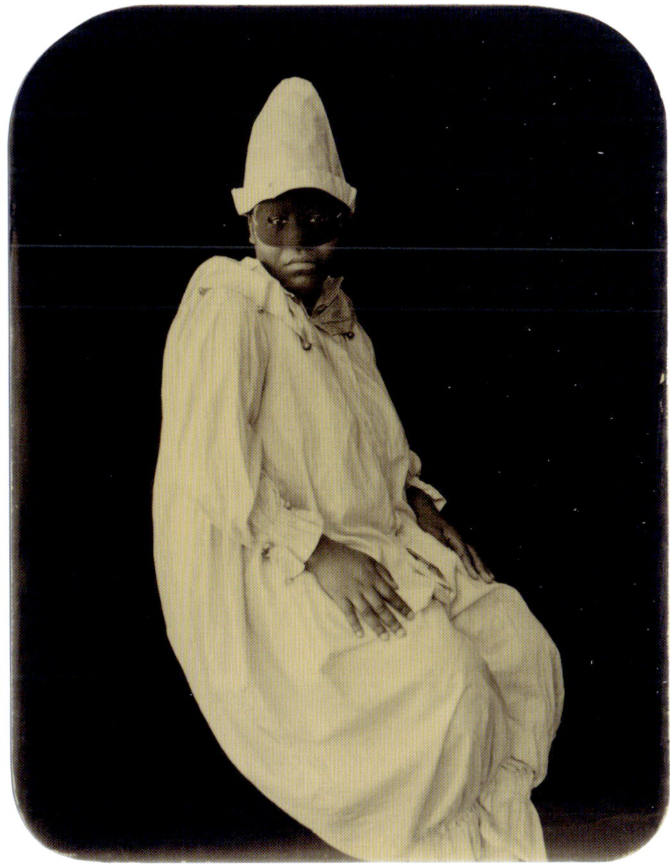

PLATE 26 **Sally Mann**, *Hephaestus*, 2008

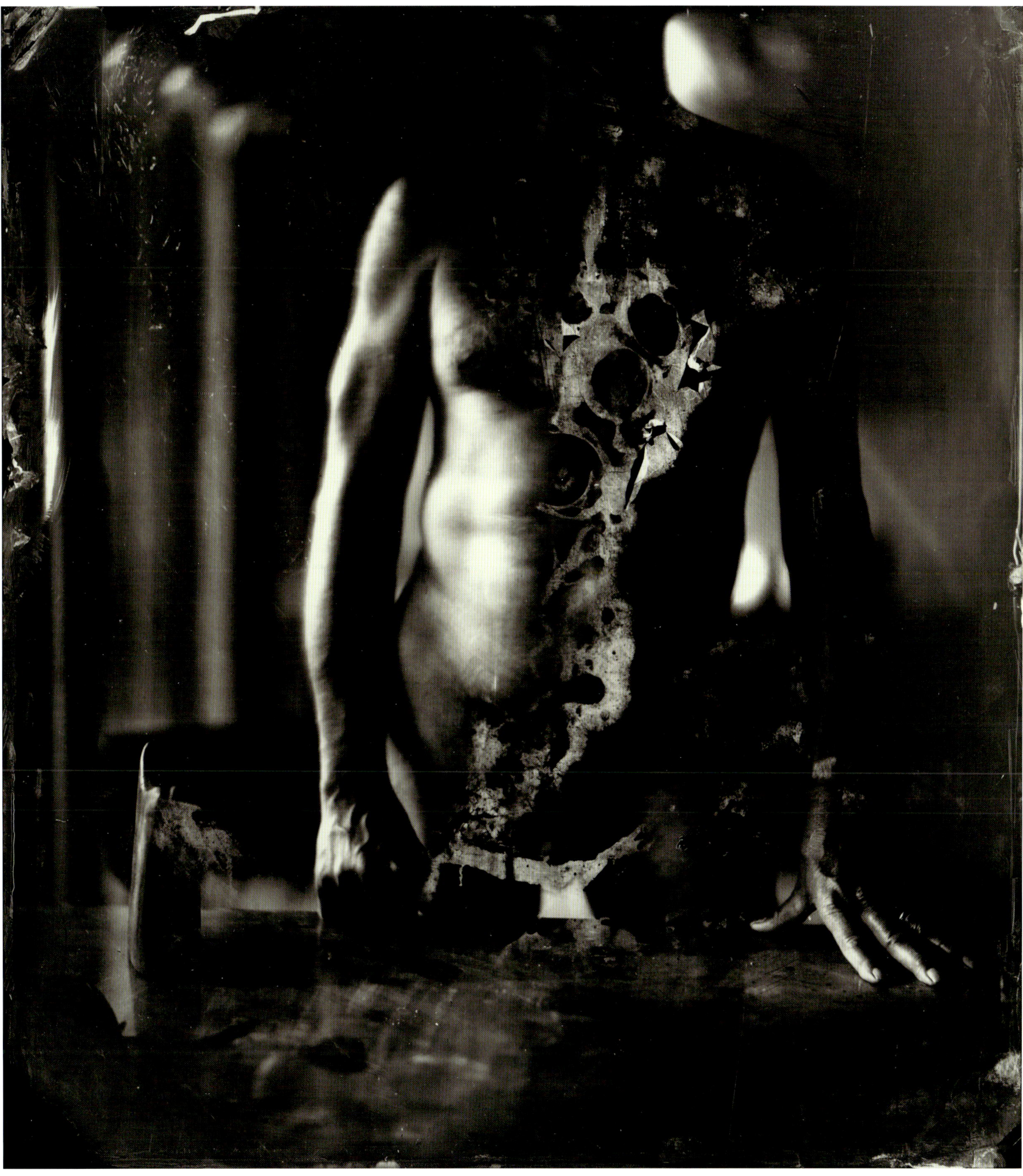

PLATE 27 **Sally Mann**, *Semaphore*, 2003

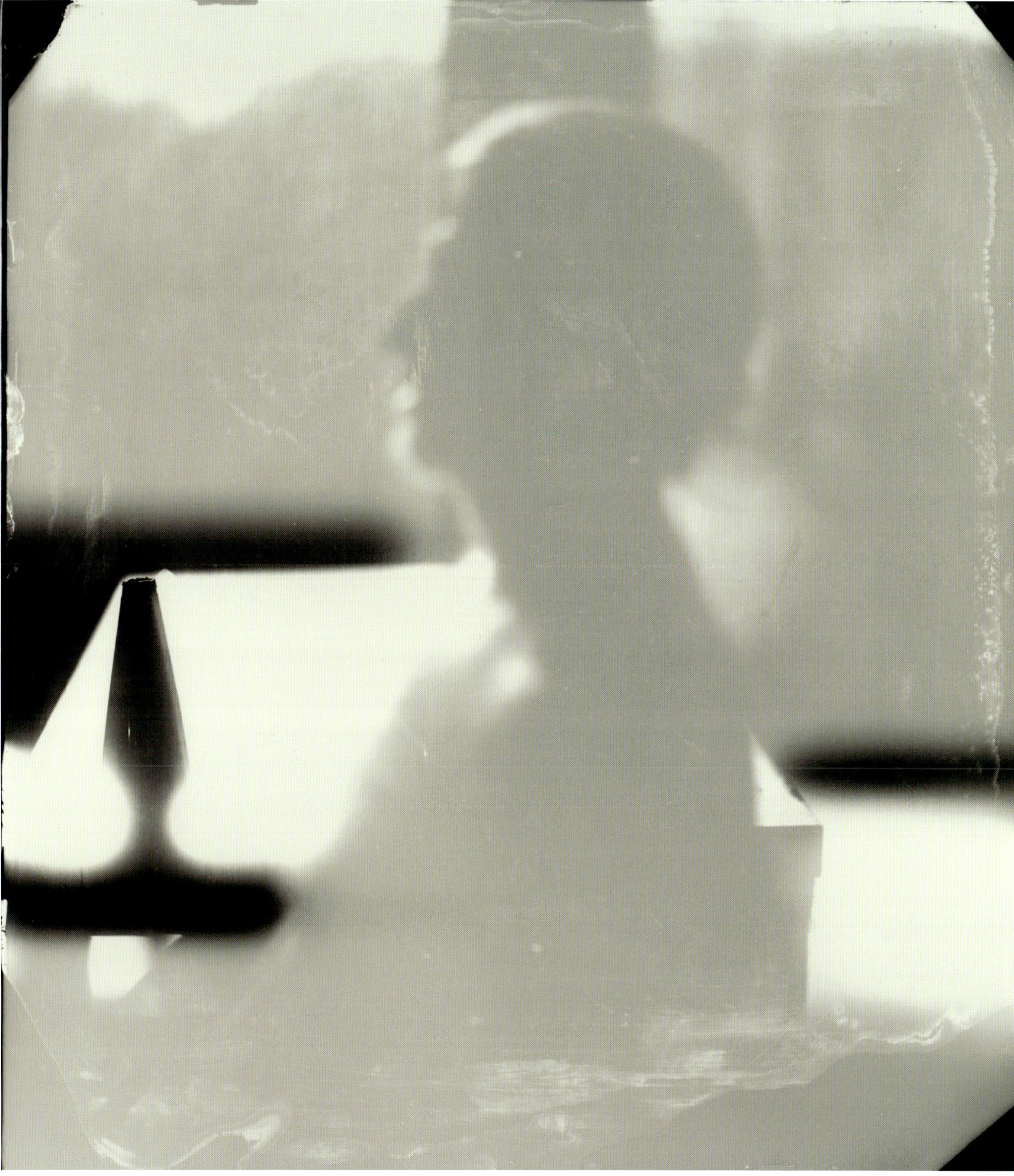

PLATE 28 **Sally Mann**, *Time and the Bell*, 2008

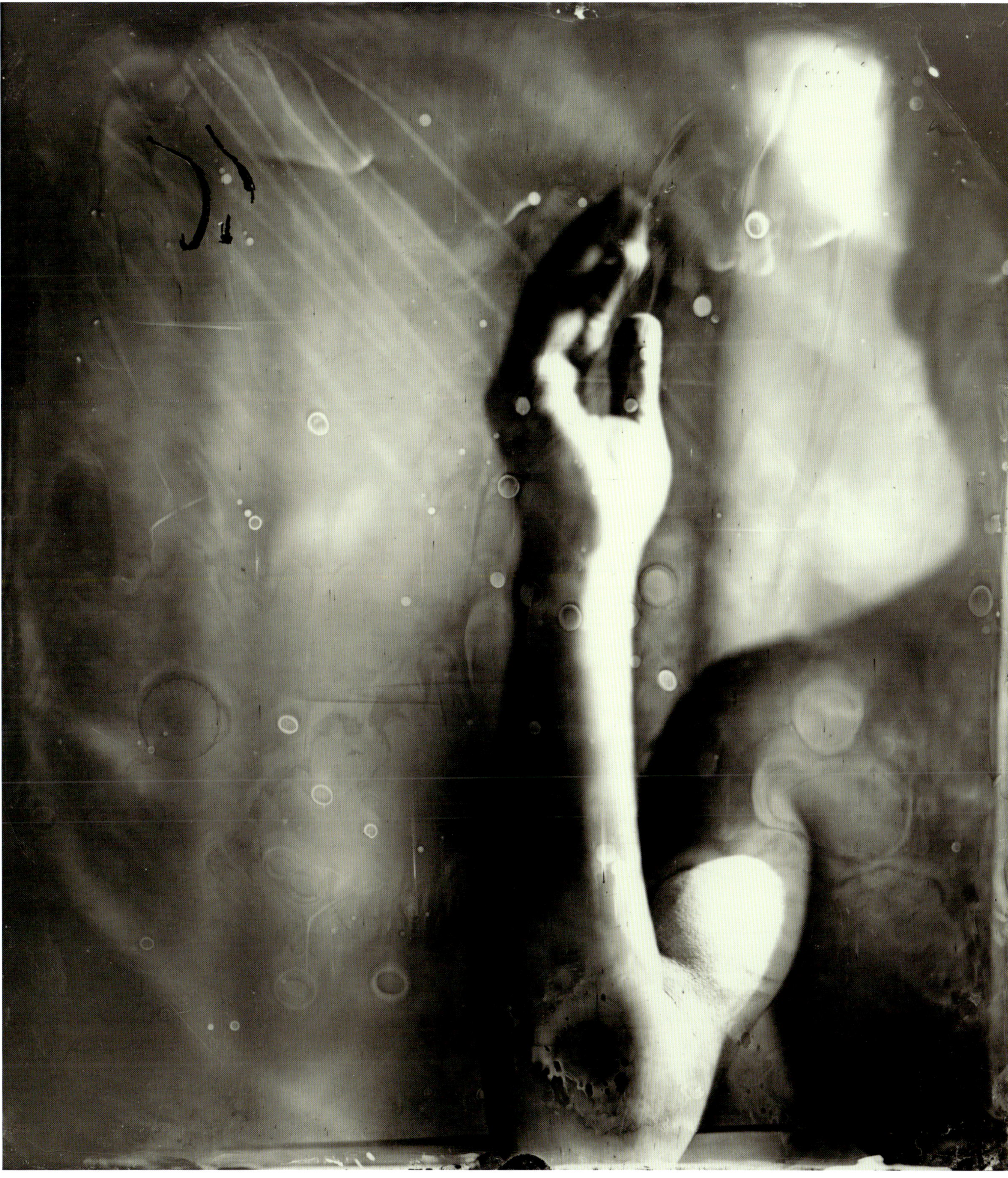

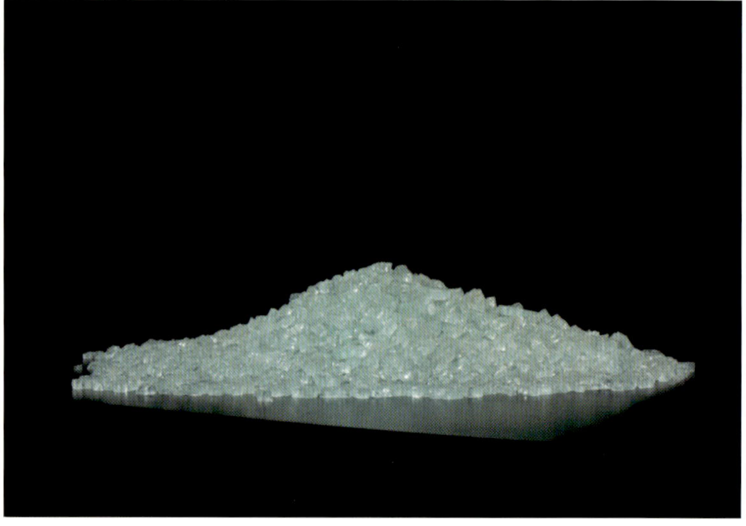

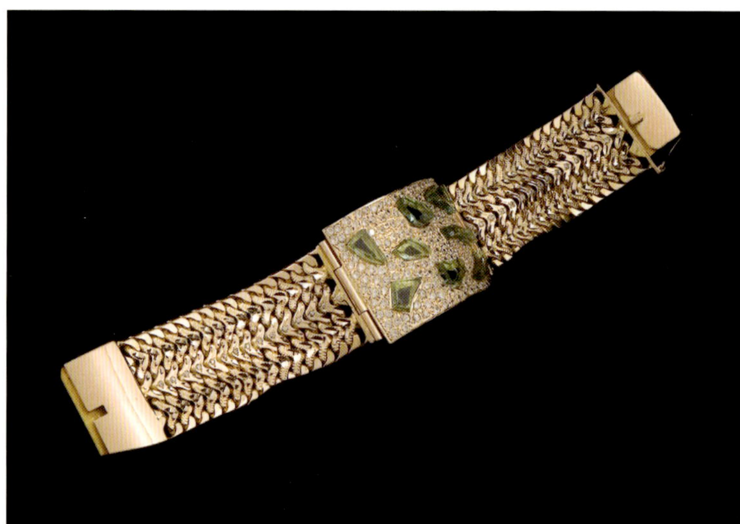

PLATE 29 **Teresa Margolles**, *Ajuste de Cuentas (Score Settling)*, 2007

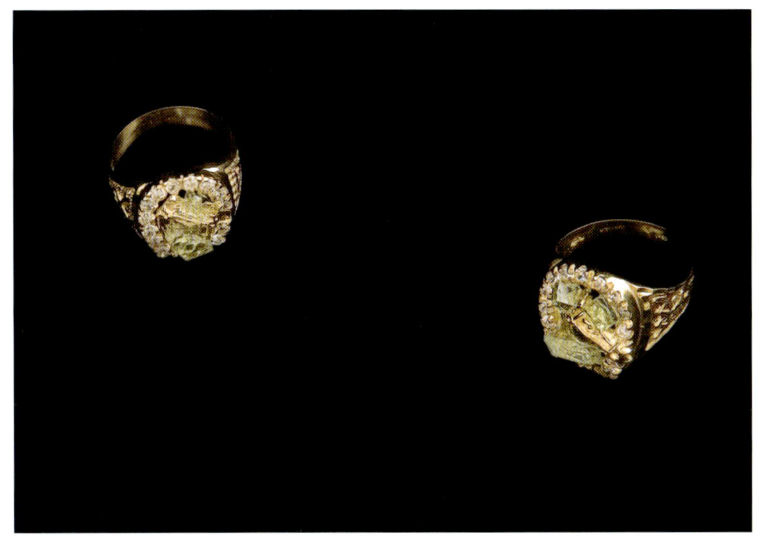

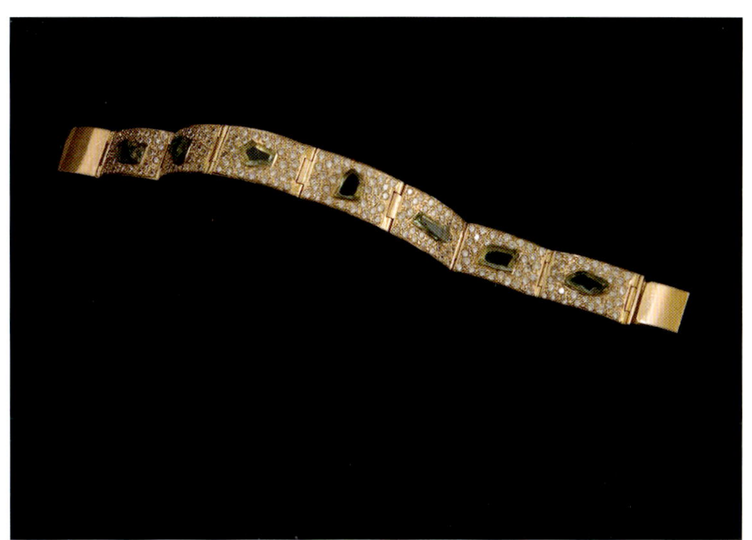

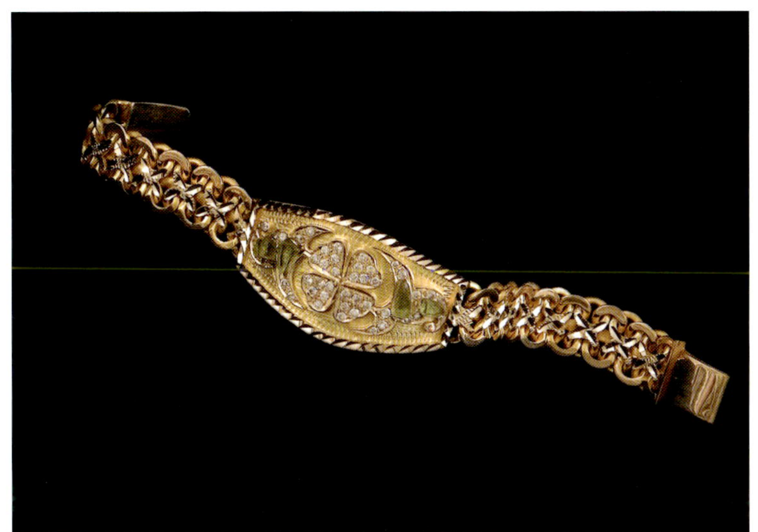

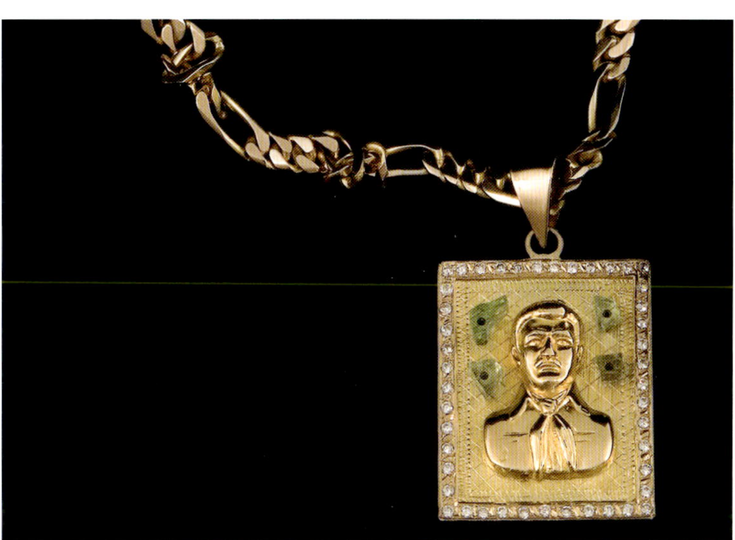

PLATE 30 **Teresa Margolles**, *Lote Bravo*, 2005

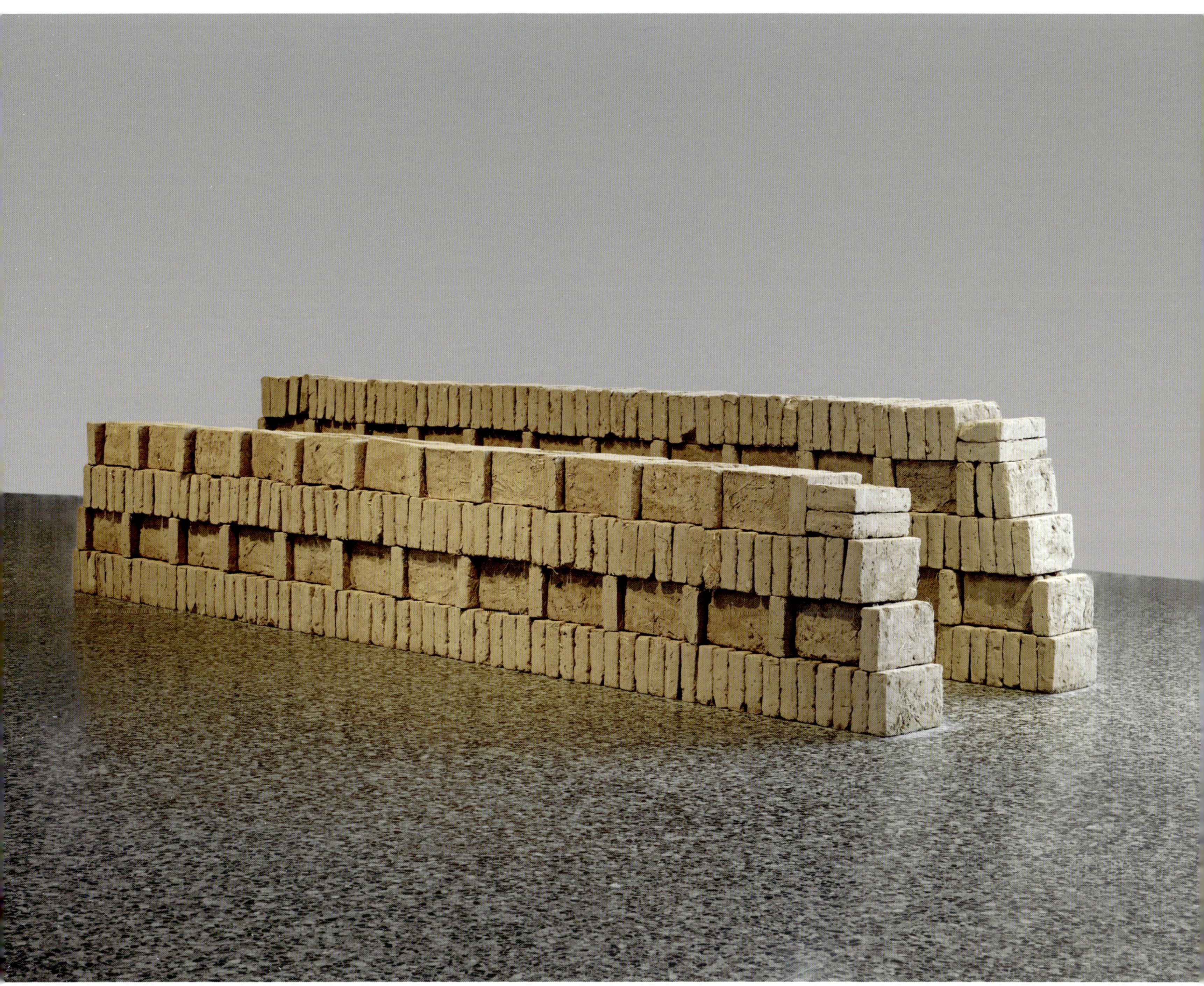

PLATE 31 **Ana Mendieta**, *Butterfly*, 1975

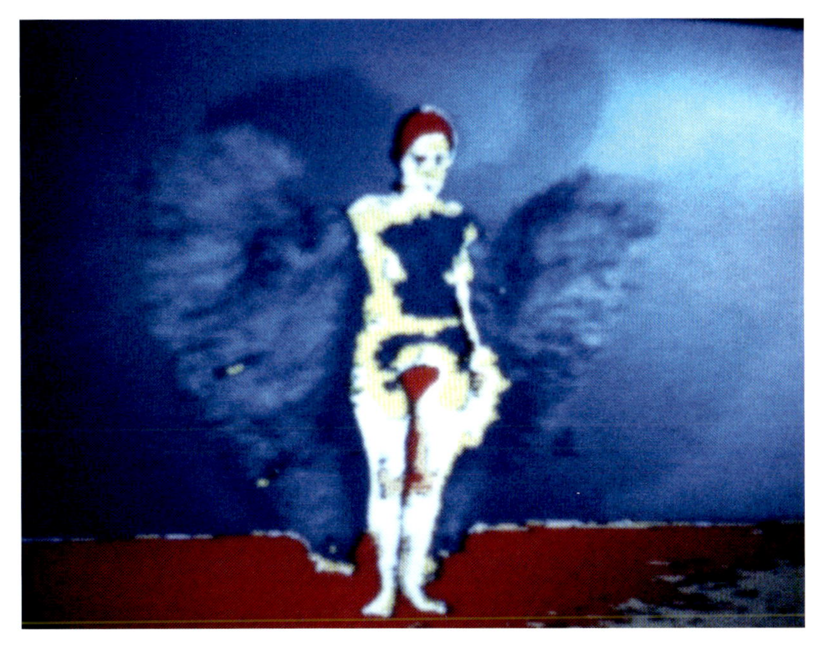

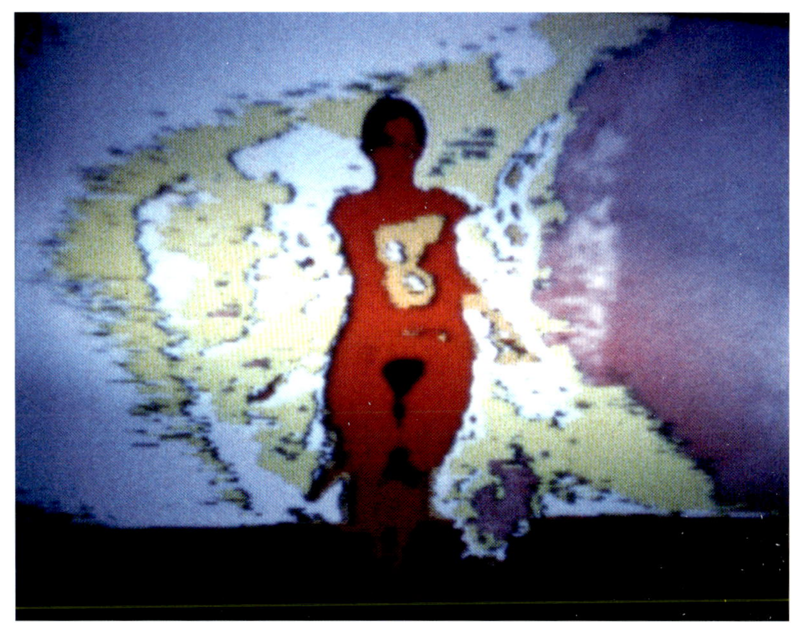

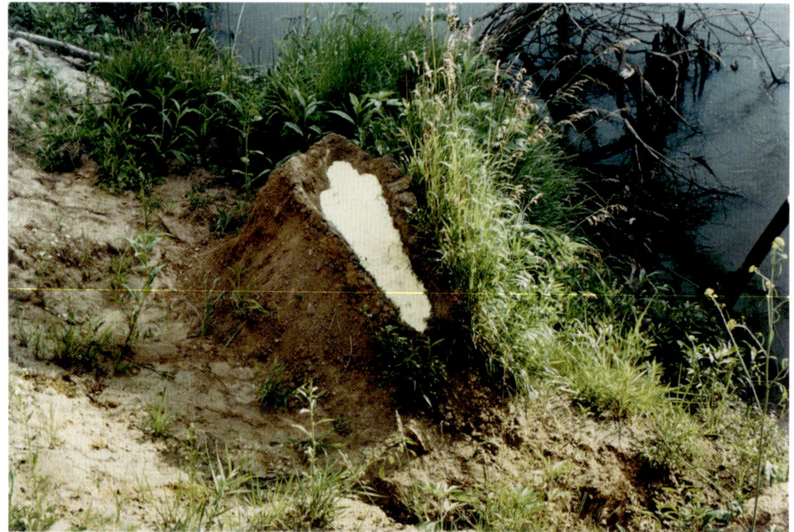

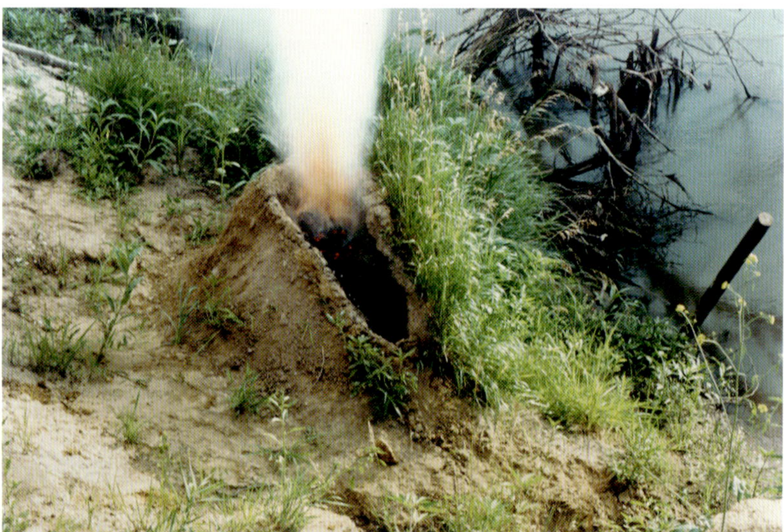

PLATE 32 **Ana Mendieta**, *Volcano Series no. 2 (Volcán serie no. 2)*, 1979

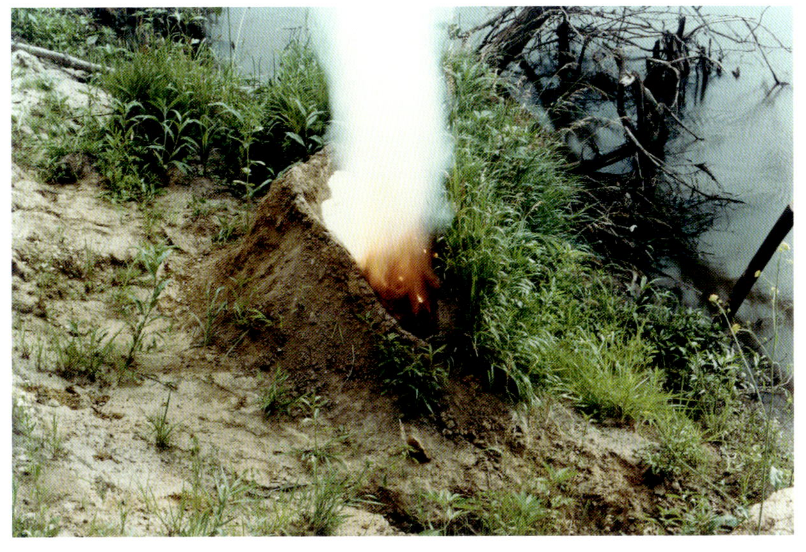
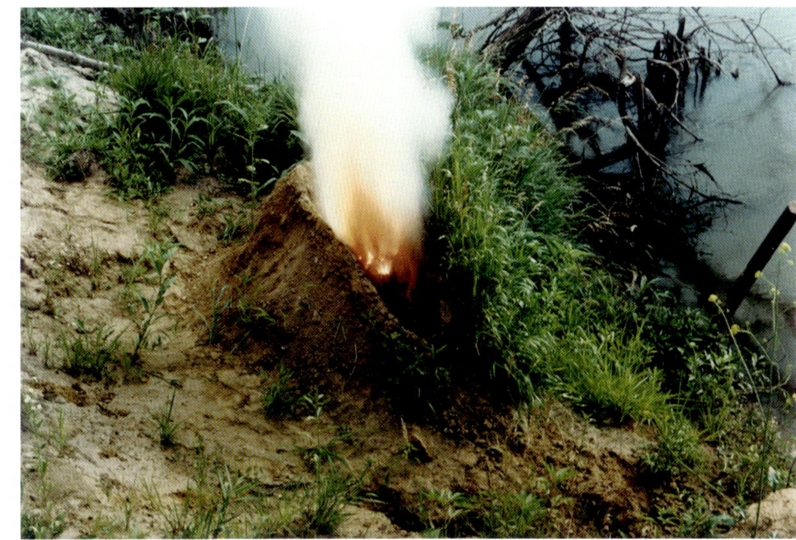
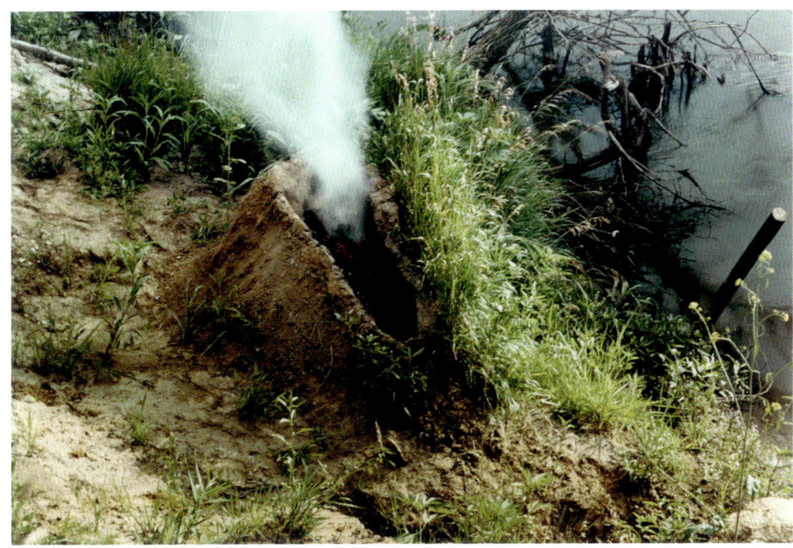
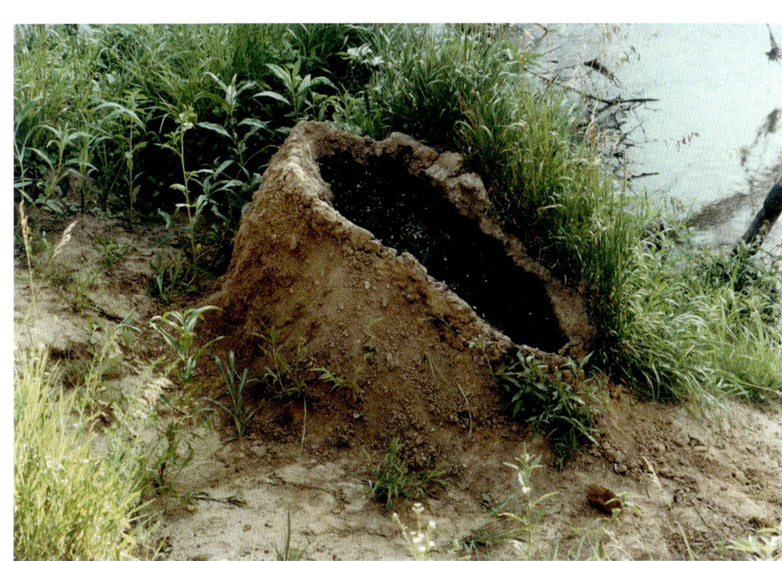

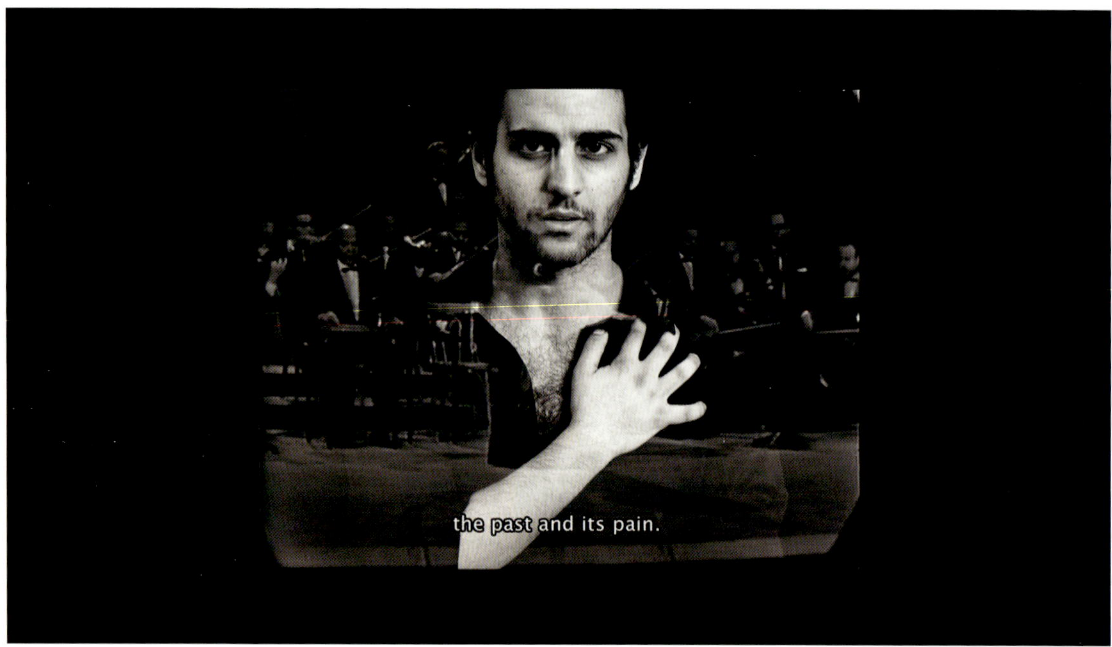

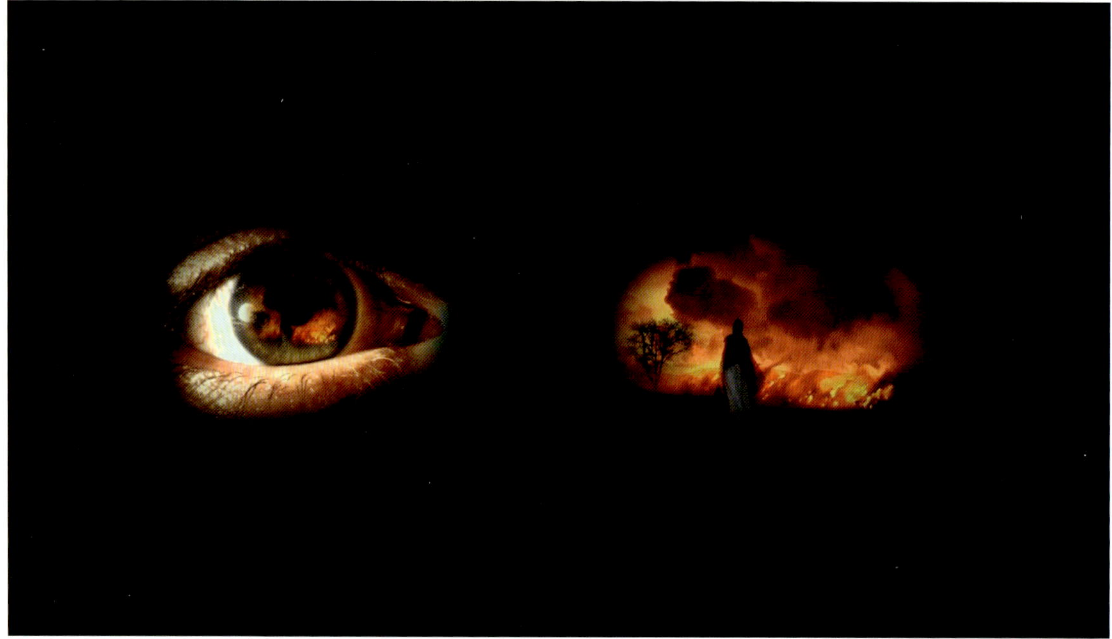

Shirin Neshat

PLATE 33, TOP LEFT *Egypt in My Heart*, 2011
PLATE 34, BOTTOM LEFT *Before My Eyes*, 2011
PLATE 35, TOP RIGHT *The Fall*, 2011
PLATE 36, BOTTOM RIGHT *Beginning of the Cold Season*, 2011

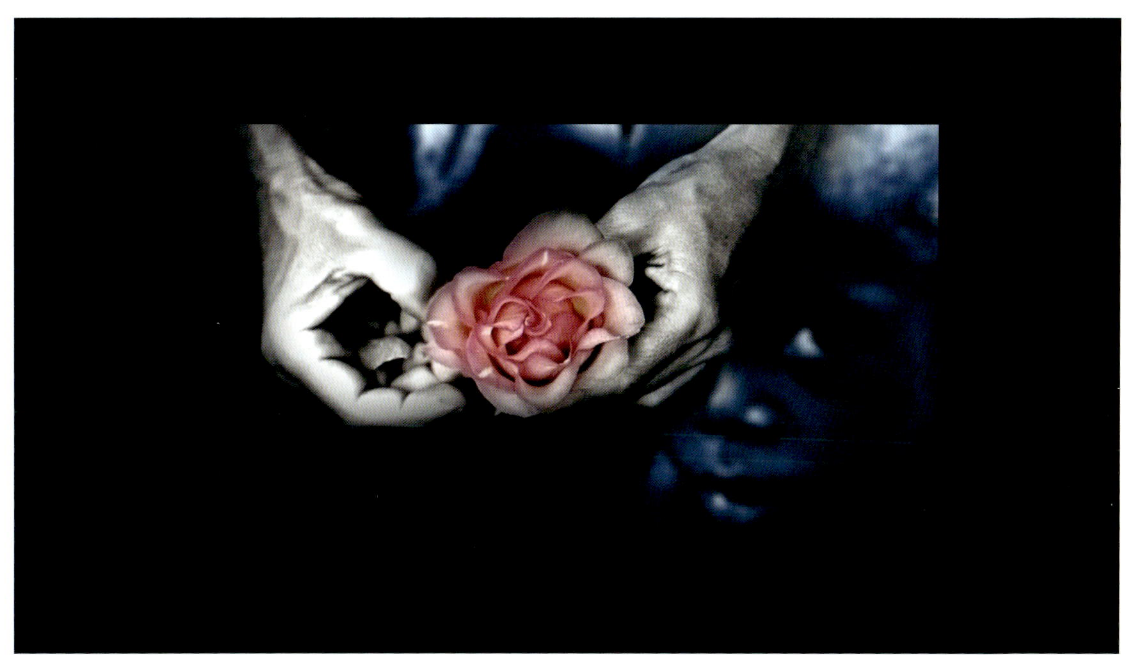

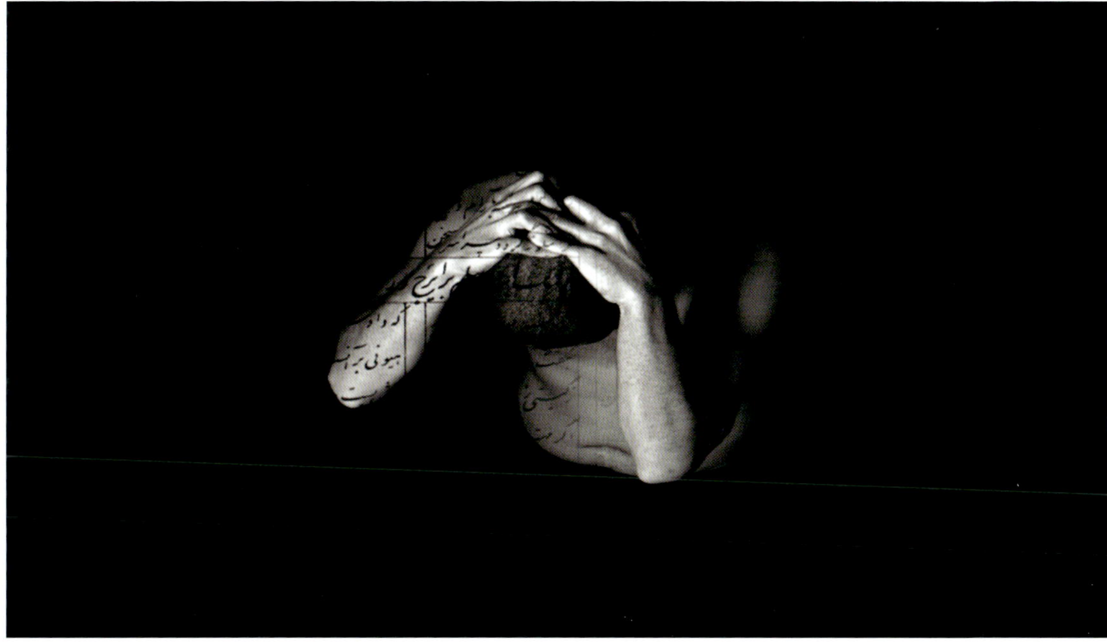

PLATE 37 **Hermann Nitsch**, *60 Malaktion MWG*, 2011

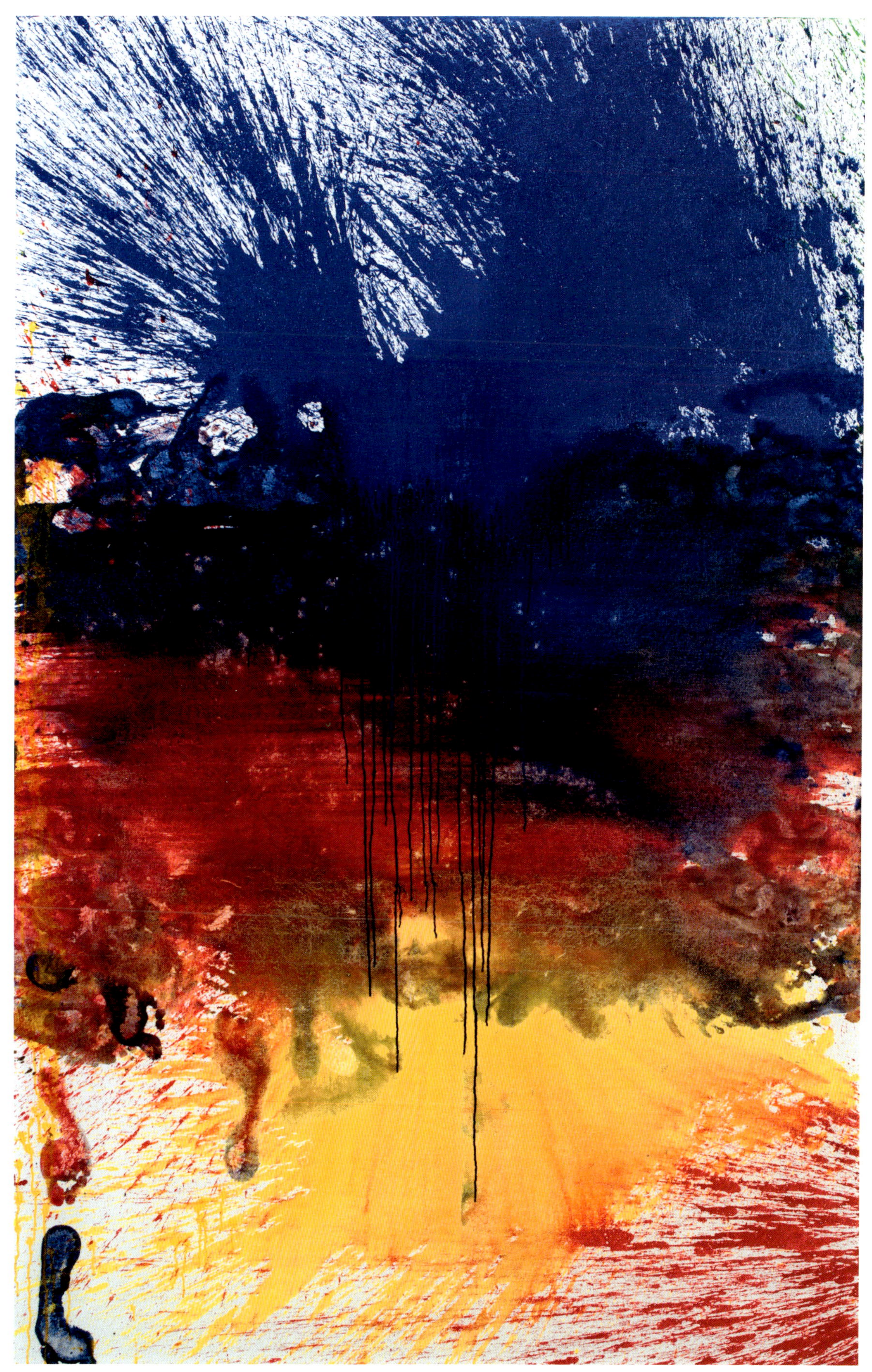

PLATE 38 **Gerhard Richter**, *Abstract Picture (Rhombus) (851-1)*, 1998

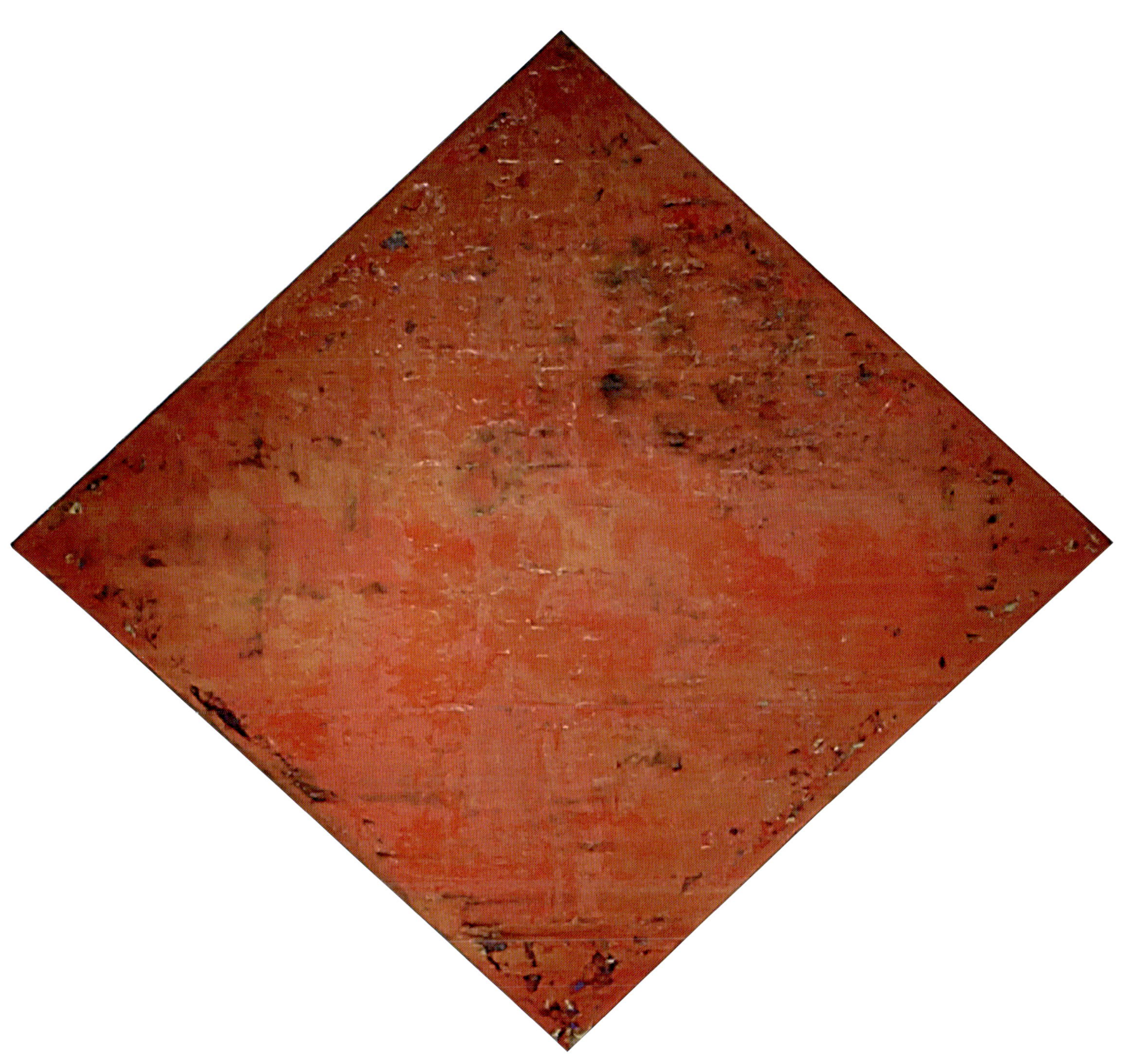

PLATE 39 **Doris Salcedo**, *Atrabiliarios*, 1992–93

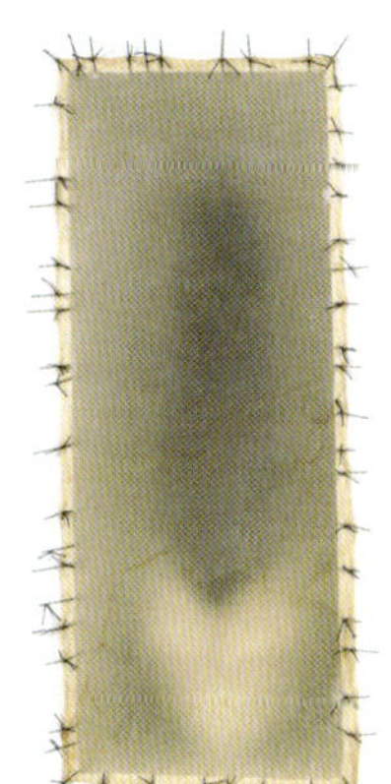

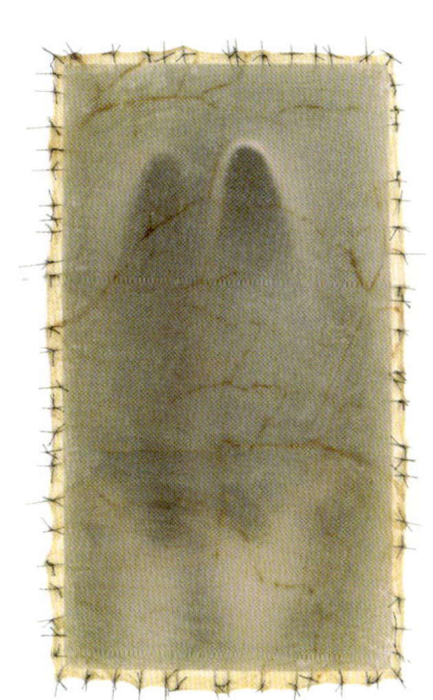
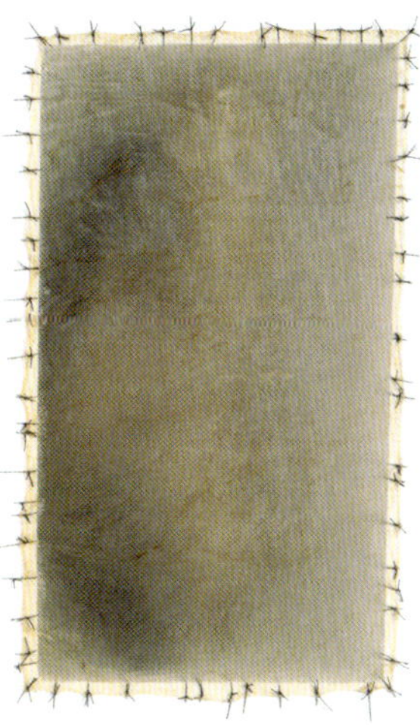

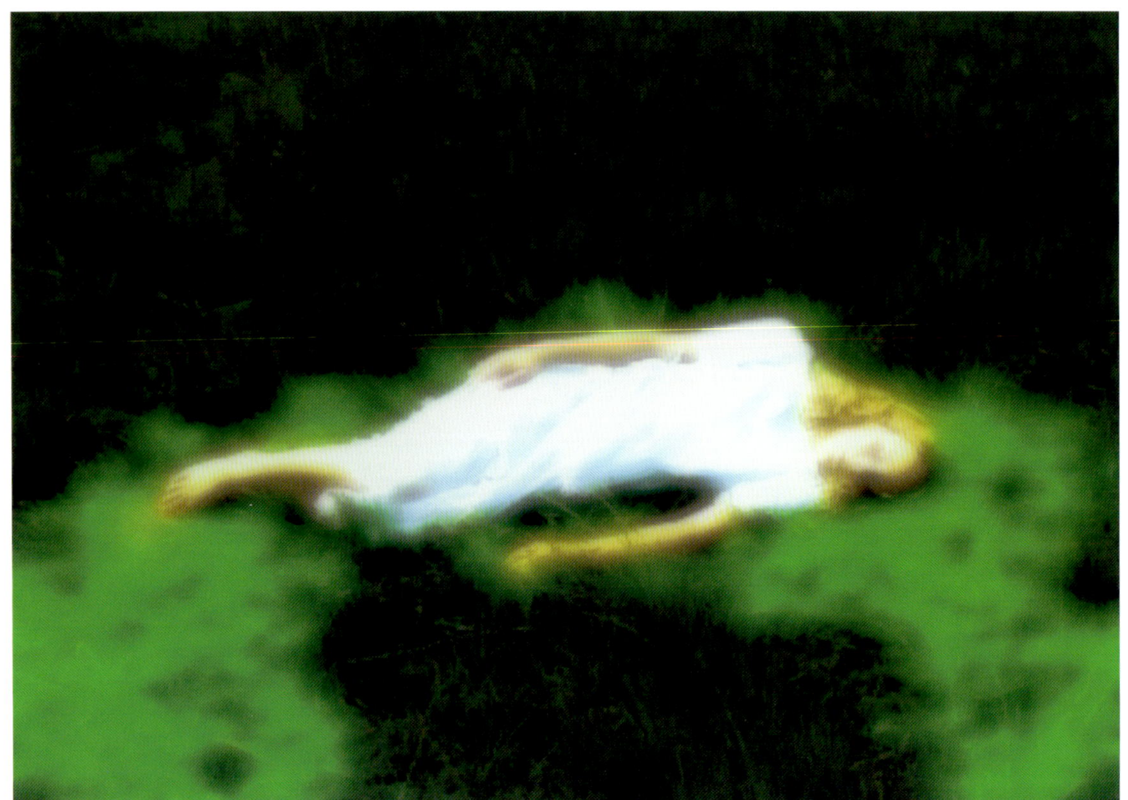

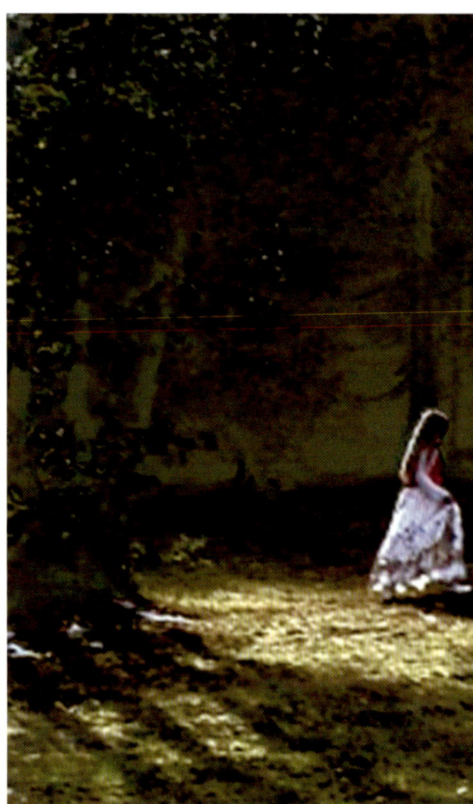

PLATE 40 **Annelies Štrba**, *Frances and the Elves*, 2003

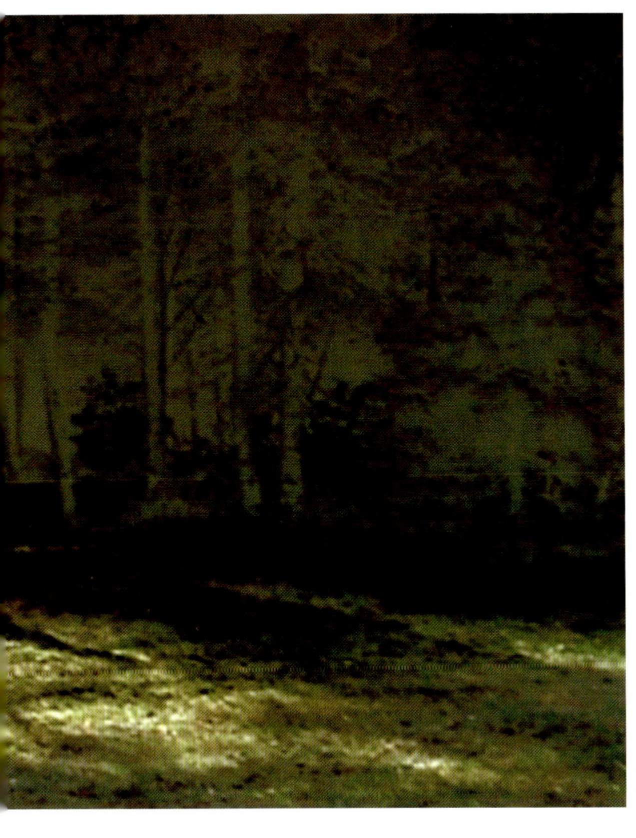

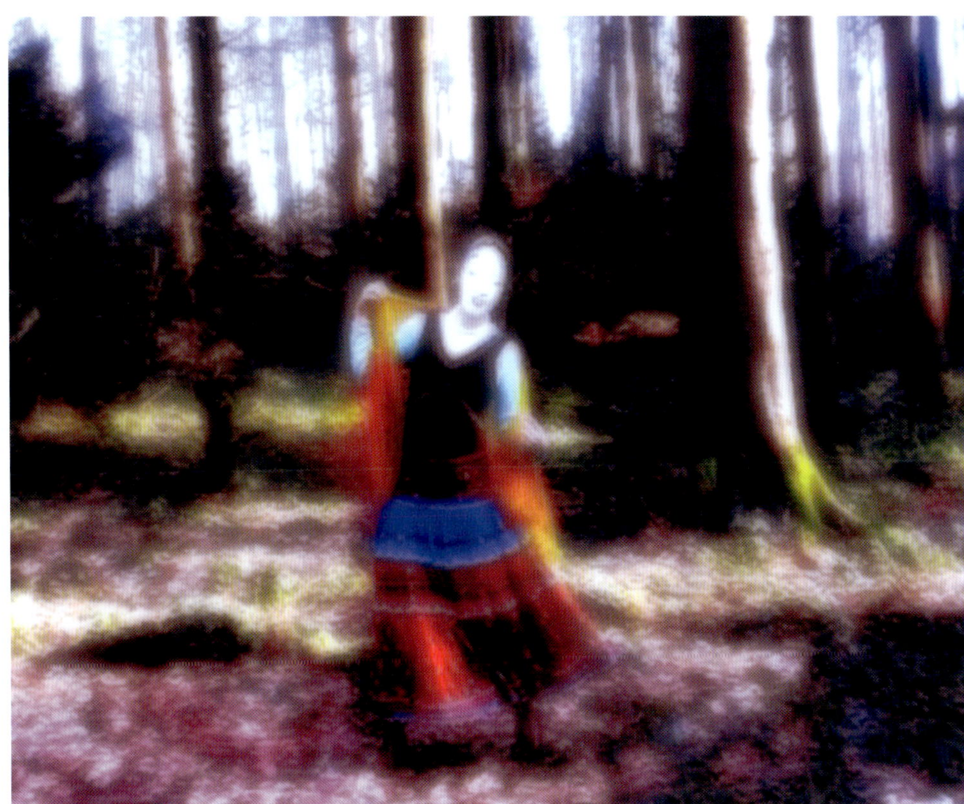

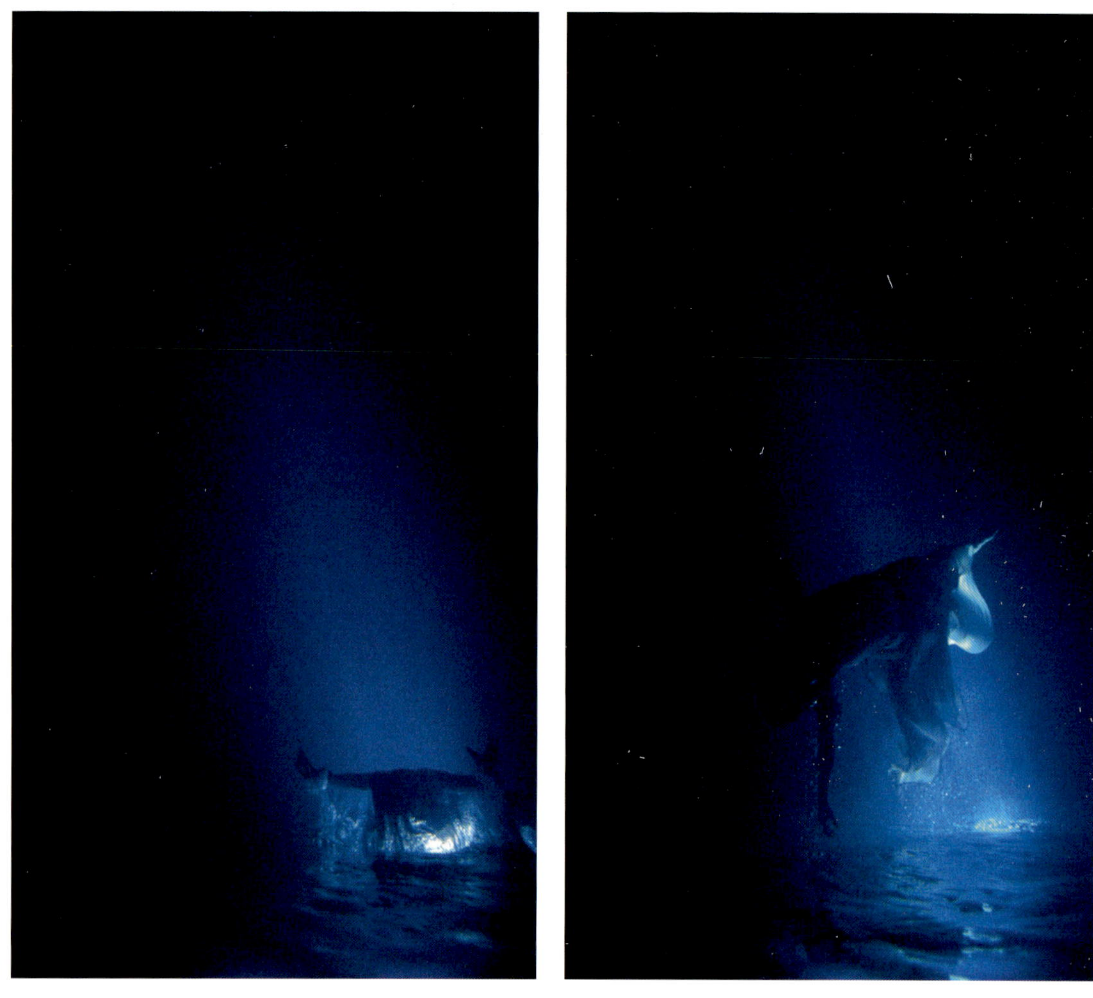

PLATE 41 **Bill Viola**, *Isolde's Ascension (The Shape of Light in Space After Death)*, 2005

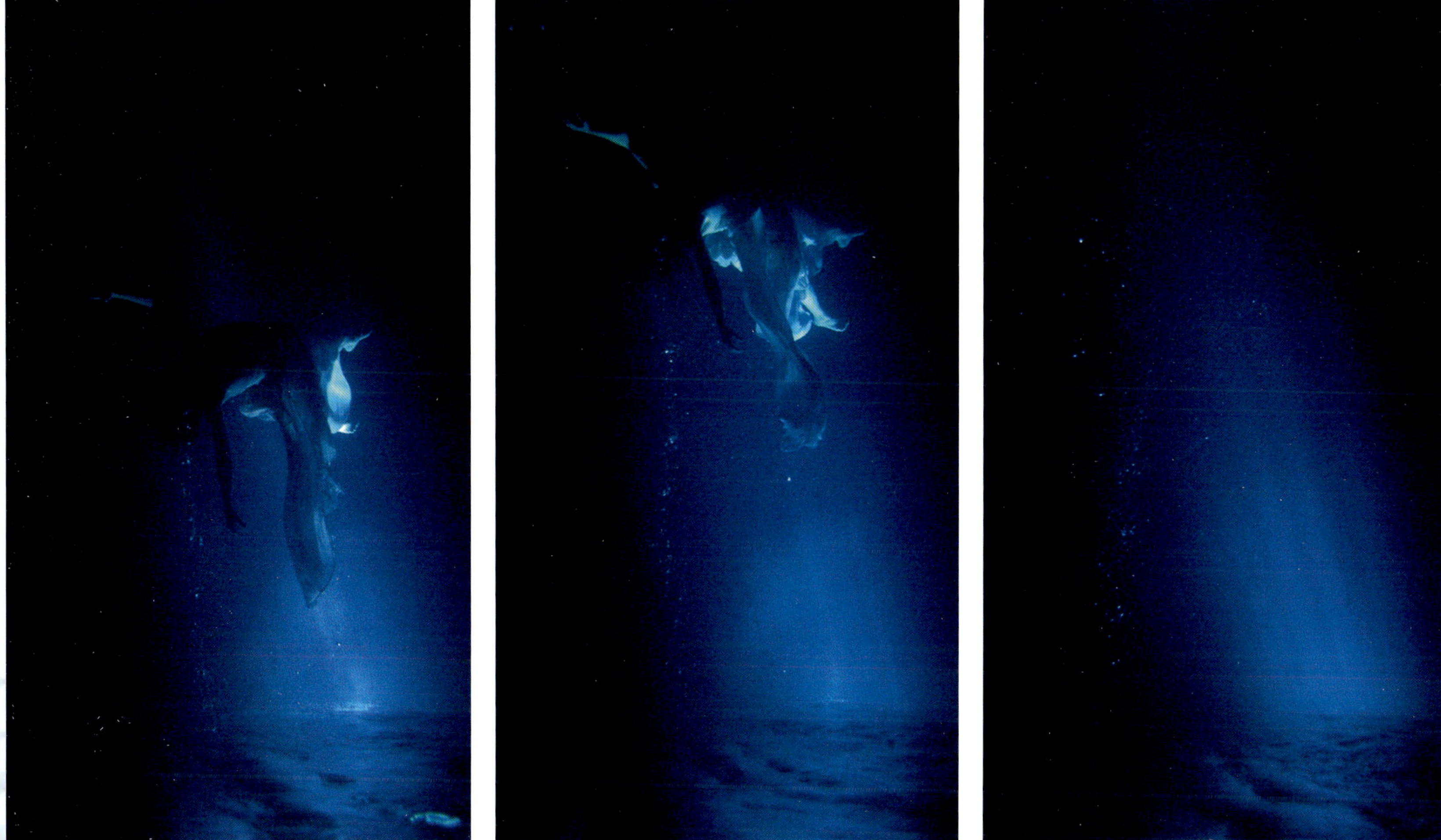

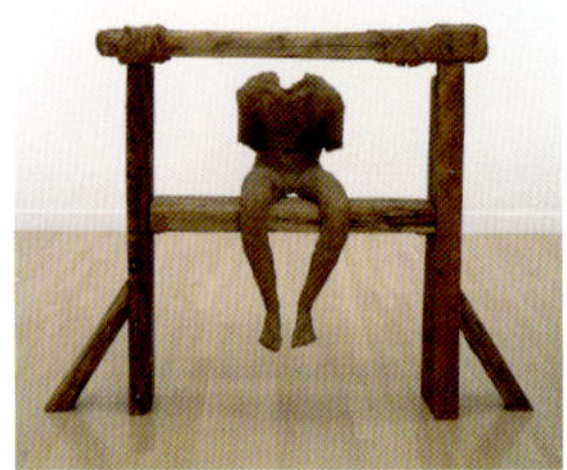

Magdalena Abakanowicz
(Polish, b. 1930)
DYBY, 1993
Wood, burlap and resin, 63 x 82⅝ x 25⅝ in.
Weatherspoon Art Museum, The University of North Carolina at Greensboro, Museum purchase with funds from the Tannenbaum-Sternberger Foundation in honor of Leah Louise Tannenbaum, 2000
PLATE 1

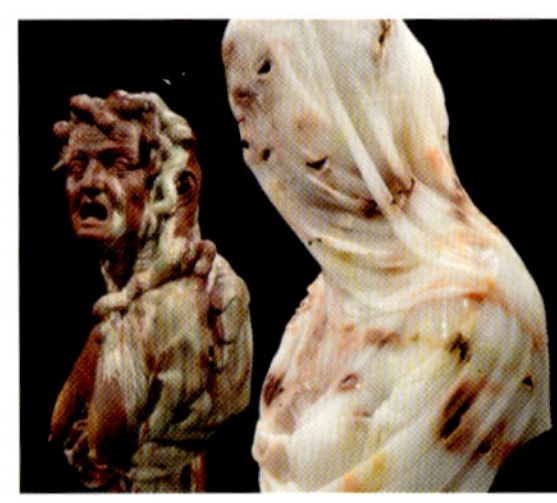

Barry X Ball
(American, b. 1955)
Envy / Purity, 2008–12
Envy—Pakistani onyx and stainless steel, 23 x 17¼ x 9½ in.
Purity—Mexican onyx and stainless steel, 24 x 16½ x 11¼ in.
Pedestals: Macedonian marble, stainless steel, wood, acrylic lacquer, steel, nylon, and plastic, 45 x 14 x 12 in. each
Collection of Mike DePaola, New York
PLATE 2

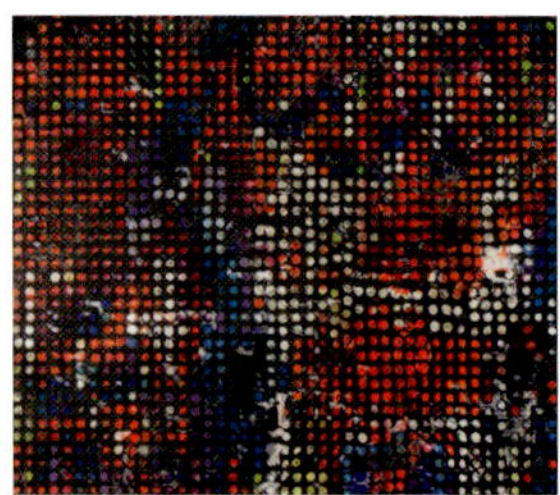

Ross Bleckner
(American, b. 1965)
A Brain in the Room, 2012–13
Oil on linen, 84 x 72 in.
Courtesy of Mary Boone Gallery, New York
PLATE 3

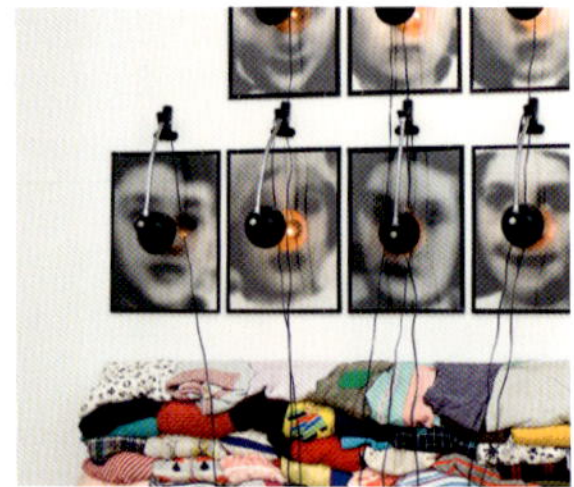

Christian Boltanski
(French, b. 1944)
Untitled (Reserve), 1989
Clothing, black-and-white photographs, and lights, 111 x 64 x 7 in. overall
Rubell Family Collection, Miami
PLATE 4

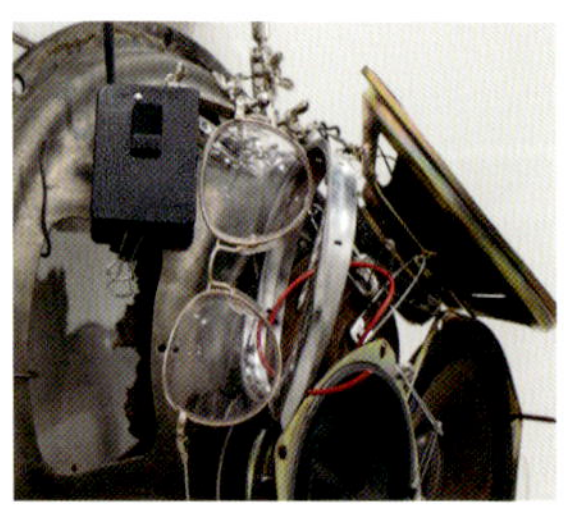

Janet Cardiff
(Canadian, b. 1957) and
George Bures Miller
(Canadian, b. 1960)
Exquisite Corpse, enfant, 2012
Mixed media, dimensions variable
Courtesy of the artists and Luhring Augustine, New York
PLATE 5

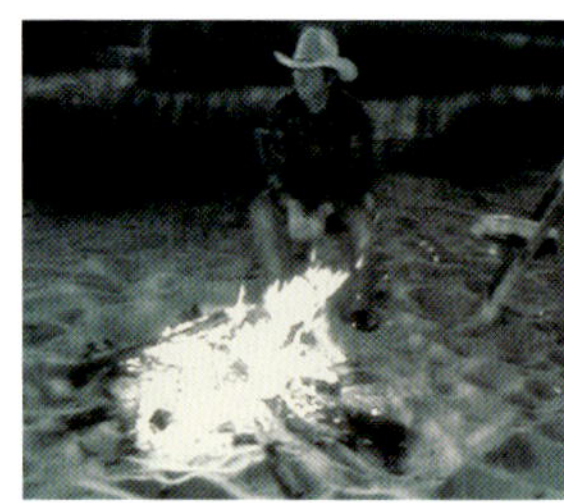

Janet Cardiff and George Bures Miller
The Muriel Lake Incident, 1999
Wood, binaural audio, video projection, and steel, 91 x 62 x 72⅞ in.; 5 minutes
Courtesy of the artists and Luhring Augustine, New York
PLATE 6

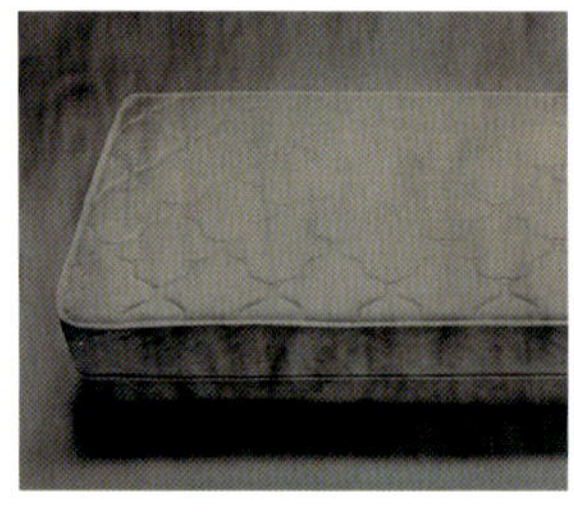

Adam Fuss
(British, b. 1961)
Home and the World, 2010
Daguerreotype, 27¾ x 42 in.
Courtesy of the artist and Cheim & Read, New York
PLATE 7

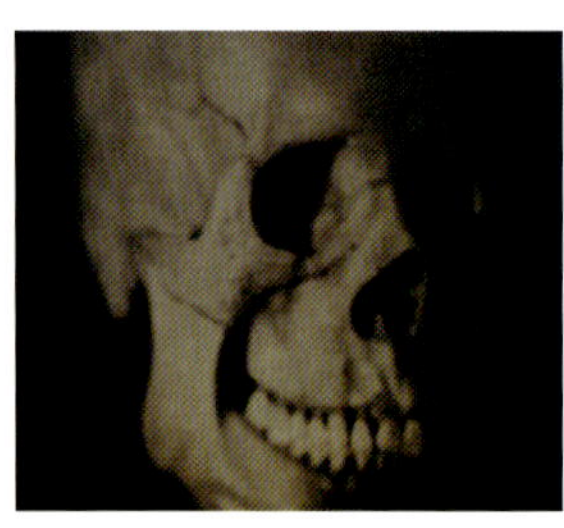

Adam Fuss
Untitled, 2002
Daguerreotype, 14 x 11 in.
Collection of Jennifer and Billy Frist
PLATE 8

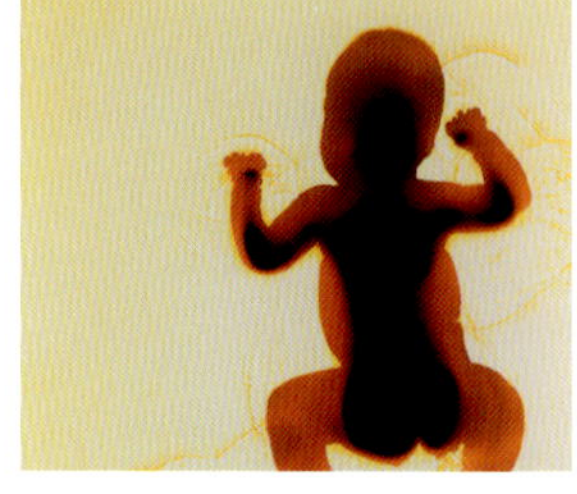

Adam Fuss
Untitled, 2006
Unique Cibachrome photogram, 40 x 30 in.
Courtesy of the artist and Cheim & Read, New York
PLATE 9

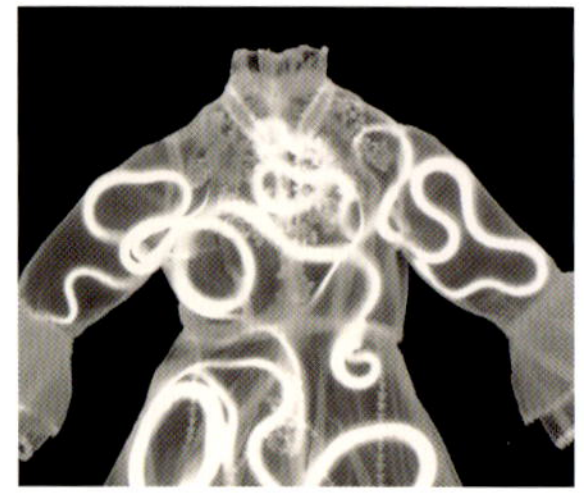

Adam Fuss
Medusa, from *Home and the World*, 2010
Gelatin silver print photogram, edition 3 of 9, 94½ x 56¾ in.
Courtesy of the artist and Cheim & Read, New York
PLATE 10

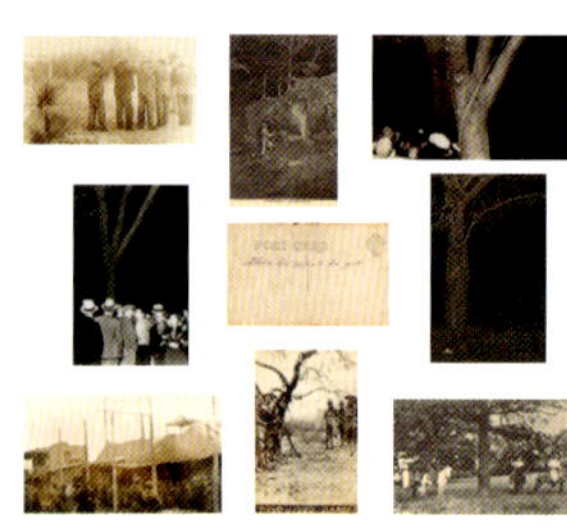

Ken Gonzales-Day
(American, b. 1964)
Erased Lynchings, 2004
15 chromogenic prints, 3½ x 6½ in. each; overall dimensions variable
Courtesy of the artist and Luis De Jesus Los Angeles
1) *Executing Bandits in Mexico;* 2) *Cowboy Justice;* 3) *Split;* 4) *Water Street Bridge;* 5) *Souvenir;* 6) *East First Street (St. James Park);* 7) *This is what he got;* 8) *Franklin Avenue;* 9) *Stain;* 10) *Tombstone;* 11) *Five in a row;* 12) *Disguised Bandit;* 13) *der Wild West Show;* 14) *East First Street #2 (St. James Park);* 15) *Tomlinson and Griffith Corral*
PLATE 11

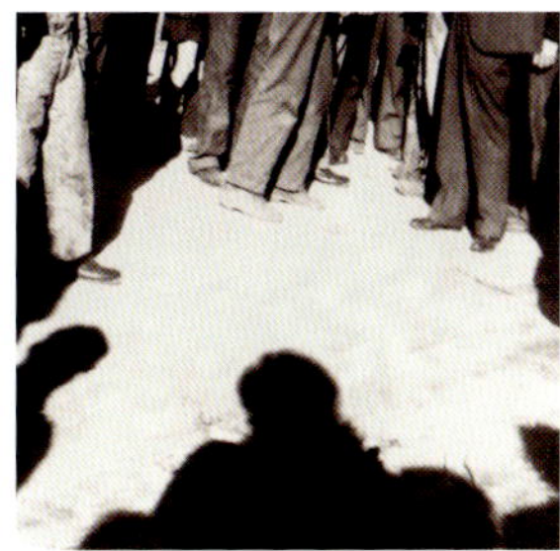

Ken Gonzales-Day
Sikeston, MO, 2013
Photograph, 60 x 38 in.
Courtesy of the artist and
Luis De Jesus Los Angeles
PLATE 13

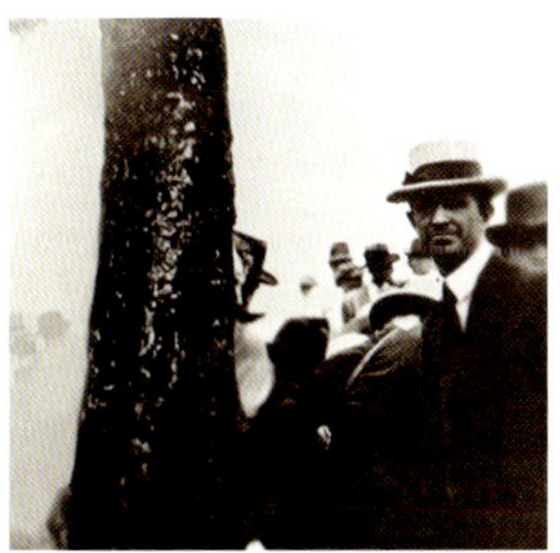

Ken Gonzales-Day
Waco, TX, 2013
Photograph, 60 x 38 in.
Courtesy of the artist and
Luis De Jesus Los Angeles
PLATE 12

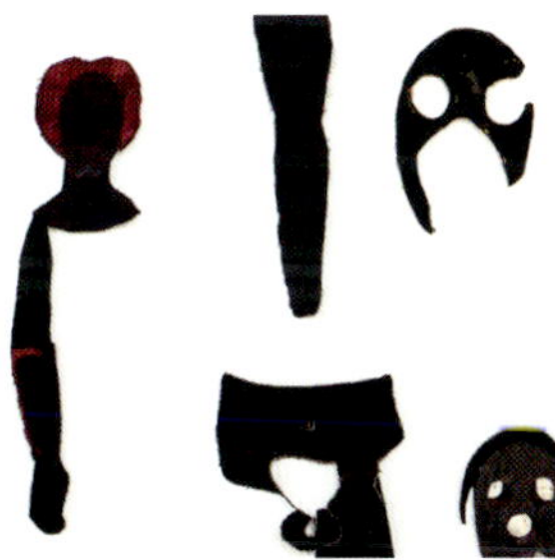

Alicia Henry
(American, b. 1966)
Untitled (Brown, Red, White, and Blue), 2012–15
Acrylic, cotton, linen, leather, wool, felt, fabric/synthetic blend, dye, thread, yarn, graphite, and colored pencils, overall dimensions variable
Courtesy of the artist
PLATE 14

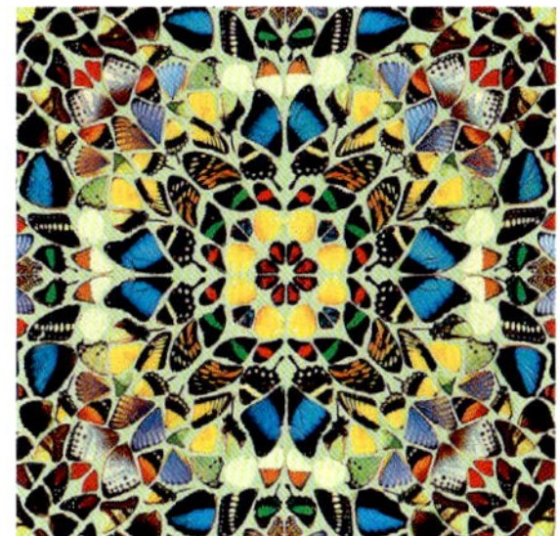

Damien Hirst
(British, b. 1965)
The Unbearable Lightness of Being, 2003
Butterfly wings on household gloss paint on canvas, 96 x 60 in.
The Broad Art Foundation
PLATE 15

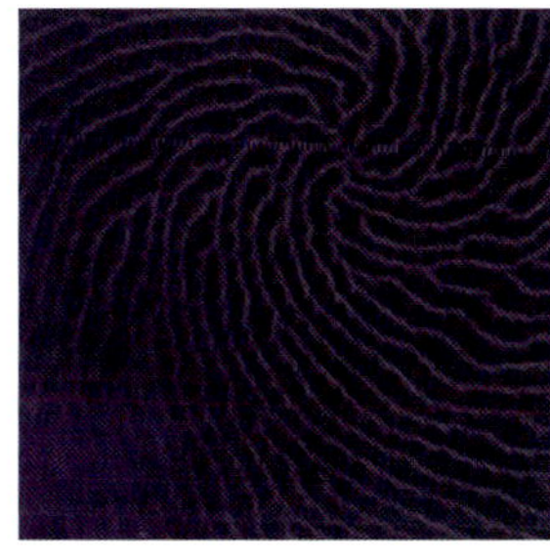

Shirazeh Houshiary
(Iranian, b. 1955)
Ode, 2013
Pencil, pigment, and black Aquacryl on canvas and aluminum, 47½ x 47½ in.
Private collection
PLATE 16

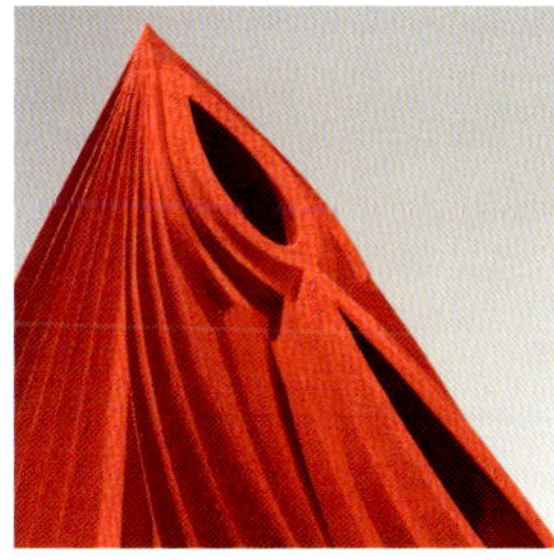

Anish Kapoor
(Indian, b. 1954)
Mother as a Mountain, 1985
Gesso and powder pigment on wood, 55 × 91½ × 40½ in.
Collection Walker Art Center, Minneapolis, T. B. Walker Acquisition Fund, 1987
PLATE 17

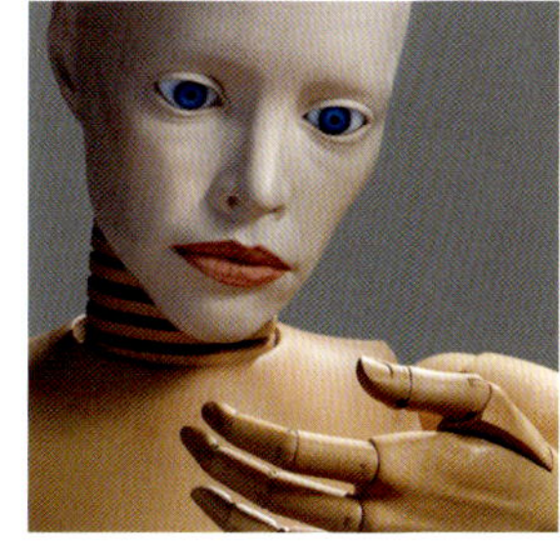

Elizabeth King
(American, b. 1950)
Pupil, 1987–90
Porcelain, glass eyes, carved wood, steel, and brass, 27½ x 7⅜ x 10¼ in.
Hirshhorn Museum and Sculpture Garden, Smithsonian Institution, Jerome L. Greene, Sydney and Frances Lewis, Robert Lehrman, and Leonard C. Yaseen Purchase Fund and Anonymous Gift, 1993
PLATE 19

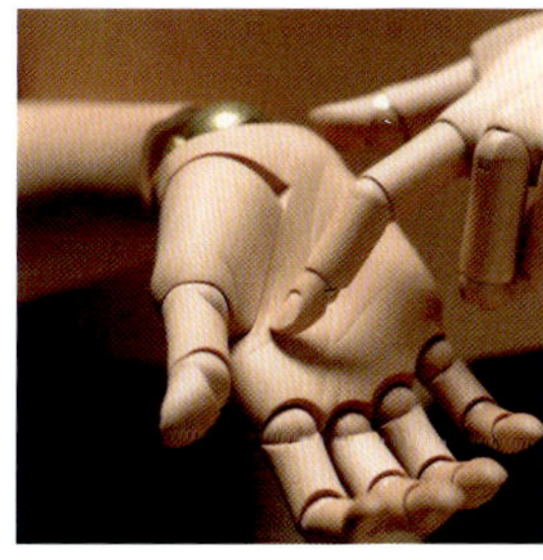

Elizabeth King and **Richard Kizu-Blair** (American, b. 1950)
What Happened, 1991 (remastered for high-definition video, 2008)
Video, two-minute loop
Courtesy of the artists and Danese/Corey, New York
PLATE 18

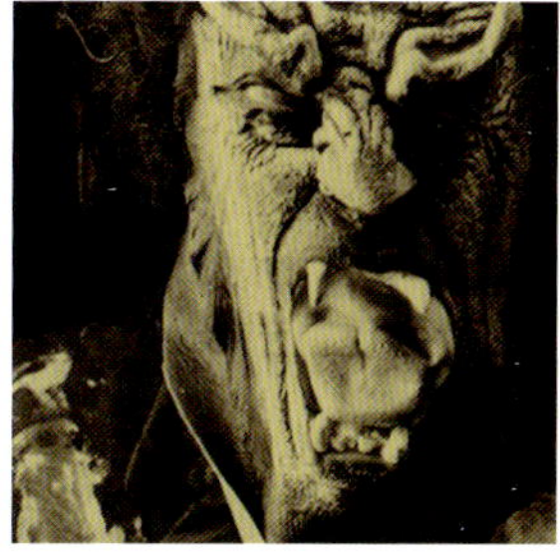

Deborah Luster
(American, b. 1951)
LCIW81, from *One Big Self: Prisoners of Louisiana*, 2000
LCIW, St. Gabriel, Louisiana, Denise Howard, doc #357771, dob 10.7.65, pob New Orleans, sentence 3 years, 1 child. No work. Halloween Haunted House
Gelatin silver print on aluminum, edition 18 of 25, 5 x 4 in.
Courtesy of the artist and Jack Shainman Gallery, New York
PLATE 23

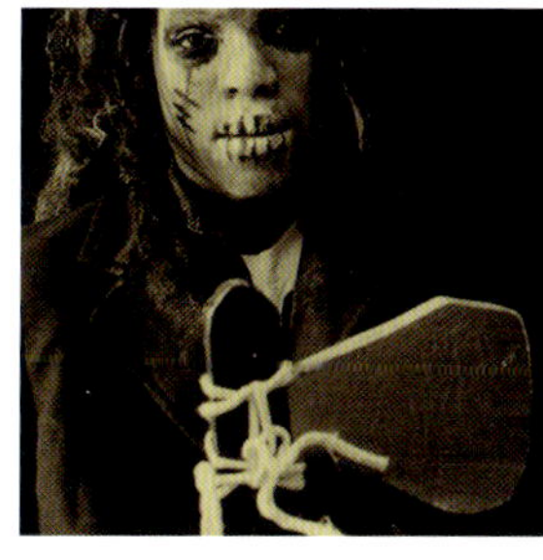

Deborah Luster
LCIW82, from *One Big Self: Prisoners of Louisiana*, 2000
LCIW, St. Gabriel, Louisiana, Geraldine Washington, doc #419988, dob 5.1.76, pob New Orleans, sentence 5 years. Work: housekeeper. Halloween, Haunted House
Gelatin silver print on aluminum, edition 17 of 25, 5 x 4 in.
Courtesy of the artist and Jack Shainman Gallery, New York
PLATE 22

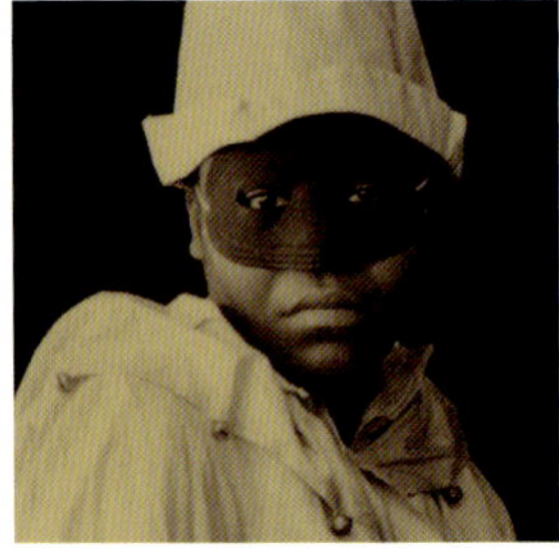

Deborah Luster
LCIW83, from *One Big Self: Prisoners of Louisiana*, 1999
LCIW, St. Gabriel, Louisiana, doc #298170, dob 7.26.68, pob New Orleans, sentence 7 years, 4 children. Work: chair plant. Halloween Haunted House
Gelatin silver print on aluminum, edition AP of 25, 5 x 4 in.
Courtesy of the artist and Jack Shainman Gallery, New York
PLATE 25

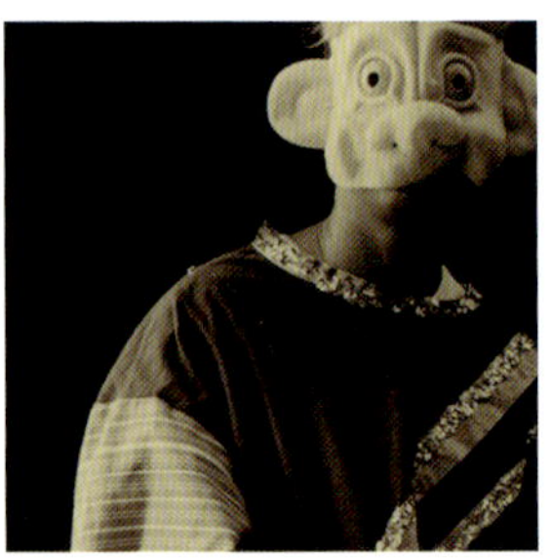

Deborah Luster
LCIW85, from *One Big Self: Prisoners of Louisiana*, 2000
LCIW, St. Gabriel, Louisiana, Concita Dixon, doc #271189, dob 5.23.68, pob. Bossier City, sentence LIFE, 2 children. Work: inner yard. Halloween Haunted House
Gelatin silver print on aluminum, edition 14 of 25, 5 x 4 in.
Courtesy of the artist and Jack Shainman Gallery, New York
PLATE 24

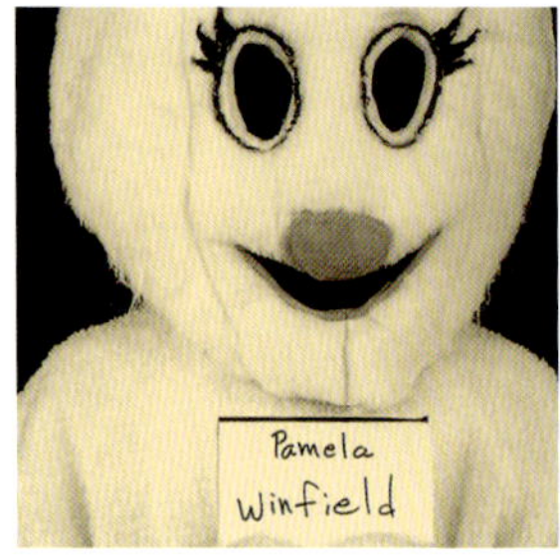

Deborah Luster
LCIW91, from *One Big Self: Prisoners of Louisiana*, 2000
LCIW, St. Gabriel, Louisiana, Pamela Winfield, doc #312197, dob 11.25.64, pob N. Kingston, RI, sentence 5 years. Work: floor worker. Easter Bunny, Children's Visiting Day
Gelatin silver print on aluminum, edition 5 of 25, 5 x 4 in.
Courtesy of the artist and Jack Shainman Gallery, New York
PLATE 21

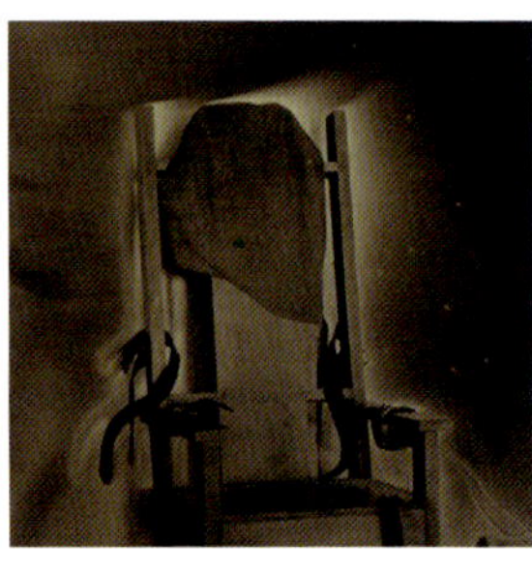

Deborah Luster
LSP143, from *One Big Self: Prisoners of Louisiana*, 1999
LSP, Angola, Louisiana. "Old Sparky," convict-built replica. From August 1941 through June 1957, Old Sparky was transported by pickup truck to Louisiana's parishes for executions.
Red Hat House
Gelatin silver print on aluminum, edition 15 of 25, 5 x 4 in.
Courtesy of the artist and Jack Shainman Gallery, New York
PLATE 20

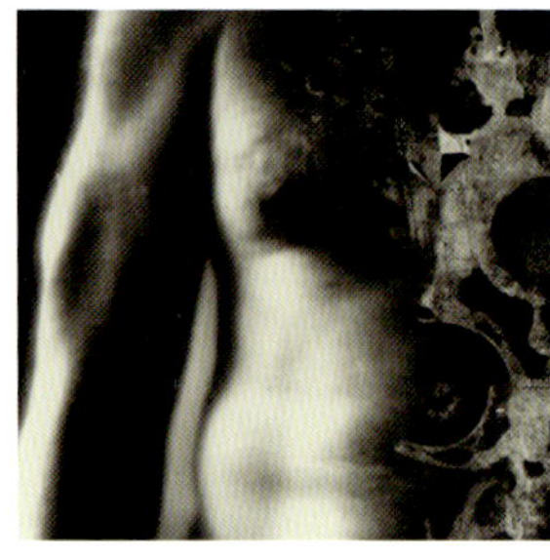

Sally Mann
(American, b. 1951)
Hephaestus, from *Proud Flesh*, 2008
Gelatin silver print, edition of 5, 15 x 13½ in.
Courtesy of the artist and Gagosian Gallery
PLATE 26

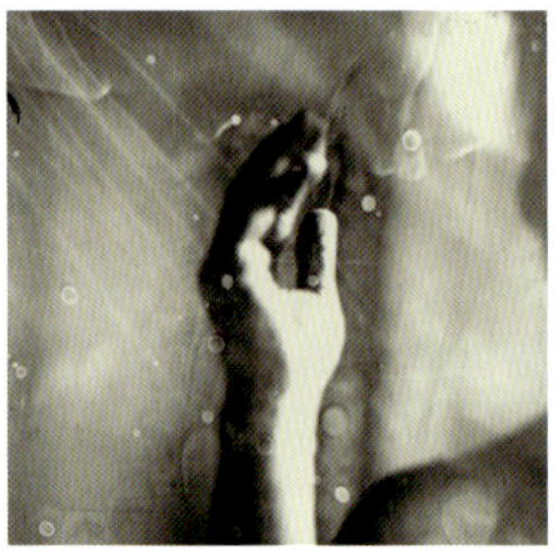

Sally Mann
Semaphore, from *Proud Flesh*, 2003
Gelatin silver print, edition of 5, 15 x 13½ in.
Courtesy of the artist and Gagosian Gallery
PLATE 27

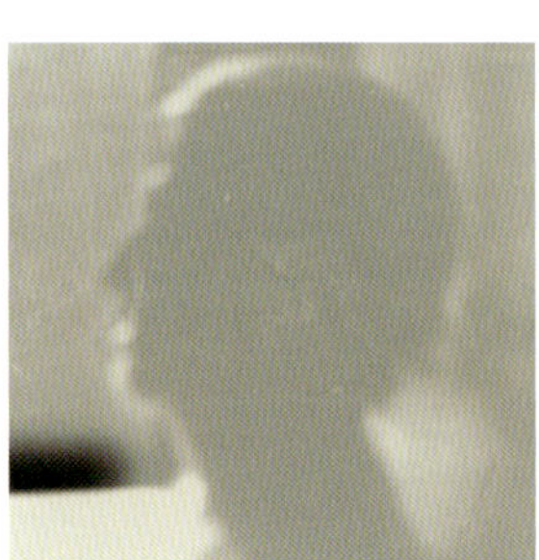

Sally Mann
Time and the Bell, from *Proud Flesh*, 2008
Gelatin silver print, edition of 5, 15 x 13½ in.
Courtesy of the artist and Gagosian Gallery
PLATE 28

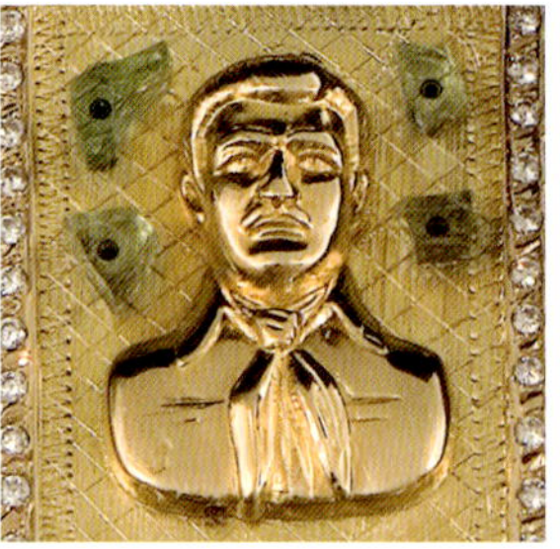

Teresa Margolles
(Mexican, b. 1963)
Ajuste de Cuentas (Score Settling), 2008
Installation of 18-karat gold jewelry and glass, overall dimensions variable
Collection of Museo de Arte Contemporáneo de Castilla y León (MUSAC)
PLATE 29

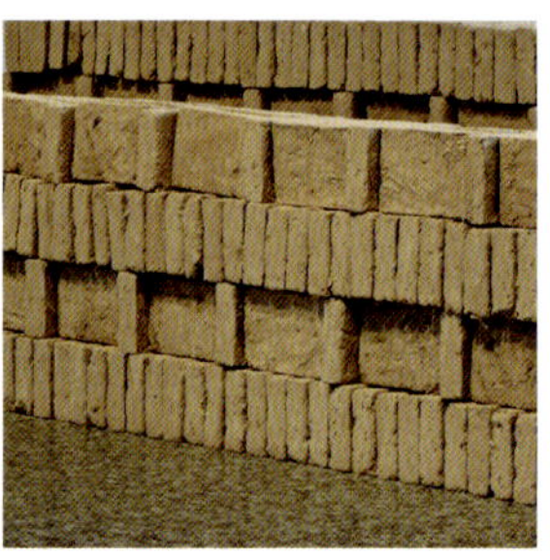

Teresa Margolles
Lote Bravo, 2005
400 mud bricks, overall dimensions variable
The Museum of Fine Arts, Houston, Museum purchase funded by the 2007 Latin American Experience Gala and Auction, Mary and Roy Cullen, Sofia Adrogué, P. C. and Sten Gustafson, Celina and Alfredo Brener, Brad and Leslie Bucher, Eduardo and Eugenia Grüneisen, Bruce and Diane Halle, Gonzalo Parodi, and Robert J. Card M.D. and Karol Kreymer in honor of Gilbert Vicario
PLATE 30

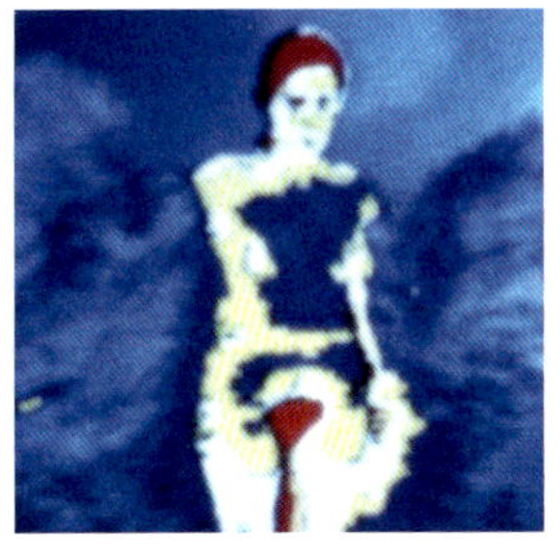

Ana Mendieta
(Cuban American, 1948–1985)
Butterfly, 1975
Super 8mm color, silent film transferred to DVD, edition of 6; 3 minutes, 19 seconds
Courtesy of Galerie Lelong, New York
PLATE 31

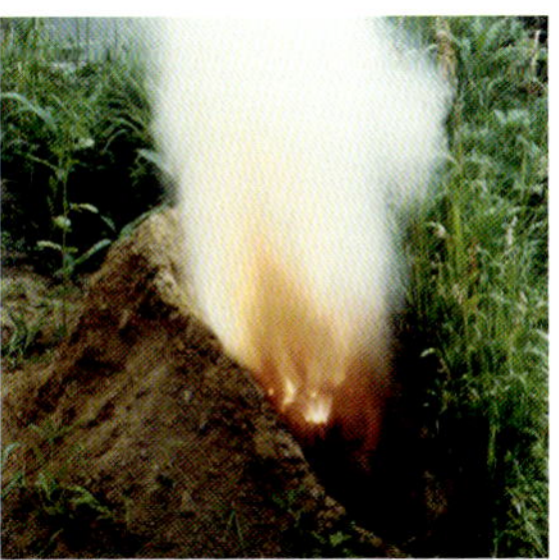

Ana Mendieta
Volcano Series no. 2 (Volcán serie no. 2), 1979 (printed 1999 Cuba)
Suite of 6 chromogenic prints, 13¼ x 20 in. each
Los Angeles County Museum of Art, Purchased with funds provided by the Judith Rothschild Foundation and the Ralph M. Parsons Fund, M.2001.55.1.1-6
PLATE 32

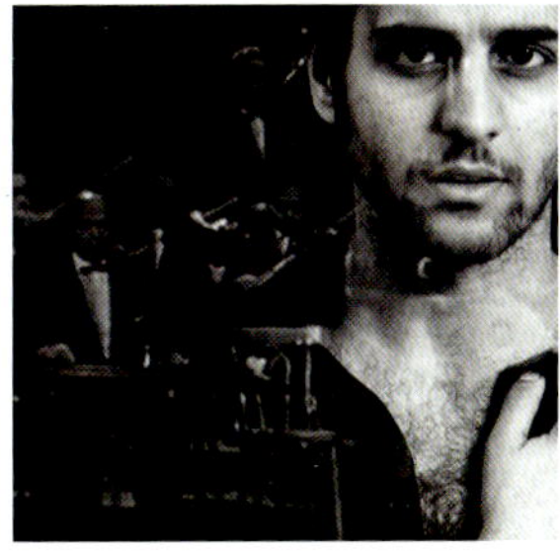

Shirin Neshat
(Iranian, b. 1957)
Egypt in My Heart, from *The Seasons*, 2011
Blu-ray Disc, a project commissioned by the *New York Times*; 4 minutes, 25 seconds
Courtesy of the artist and Gladstone Gallery, New York and Brussels
PLATE 33

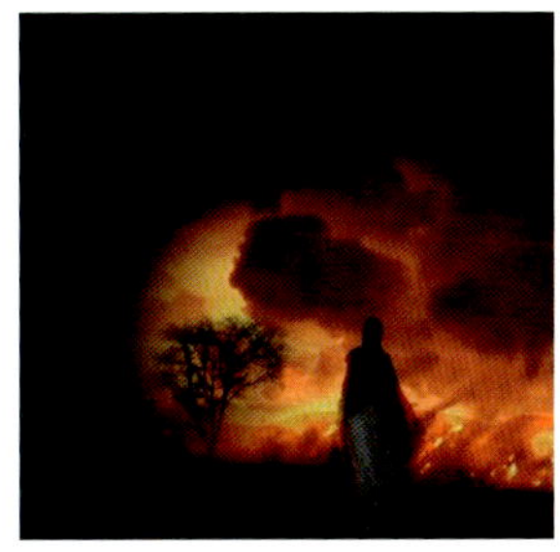

Shirin Neshat
Before my Eyes, from *The Seasons*, 2011
Blu-ray Disc, a project commissioned by the *New York Times*; 2 minutes, 55 seconds
Courtesy of the artist and Gladstone Gallery, New York and Brussels
PLATE 34

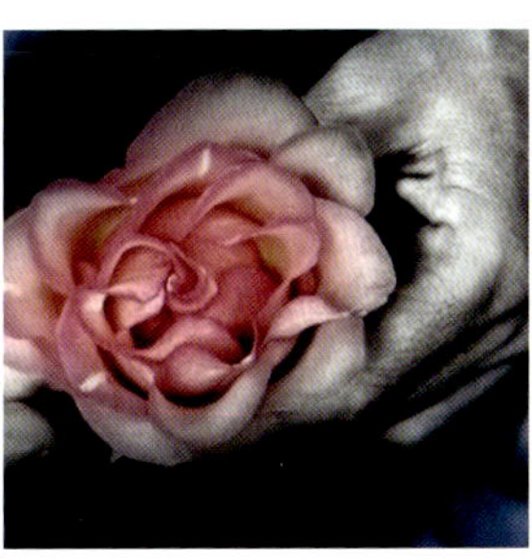

Shirin Neshat
The Fall, from *The Seasons*, 2011
Blu-ray Disc, a project commissioned by the *New York Times*; 3 minutes, 11 seconds
Courtesy of the artist and Gladstone Gallery, New York and Brussels
PLATE 35

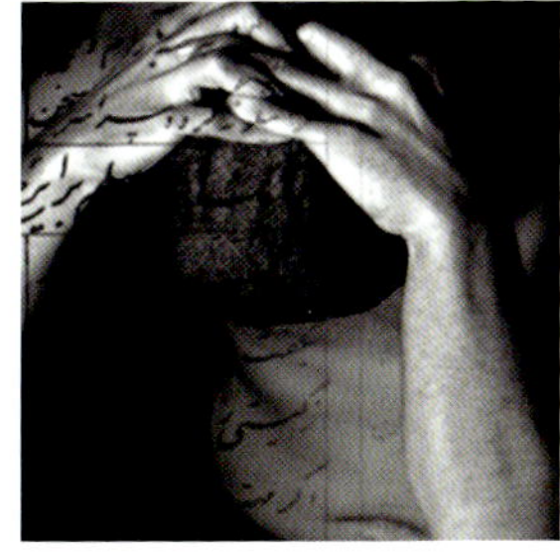

Shirin Neshat
Beginning of the Cold Season, from *The Seasons*, 2011
Blu-ray Disc, a project commissioned by the *New York Times*; 4 minutes, 34 seconds
Courtesy of the artist and Gladstone Gallery, New York and Brussels
PLATE 36

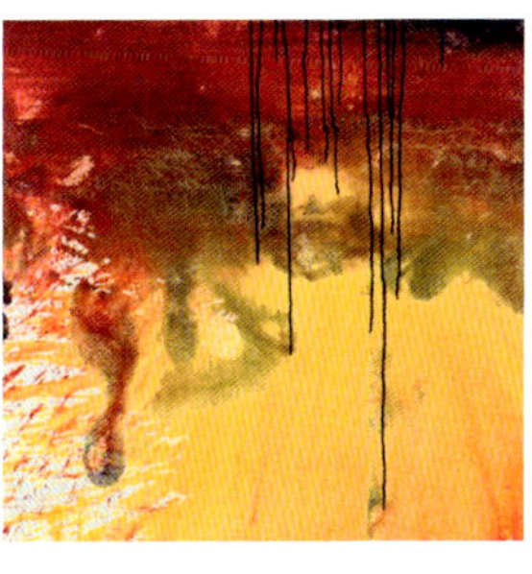

Hermann Nitsch
(Austrian, b. 1938)
60 Malaktion MWG, 2011
Acrylic on jute, 88 x 55 in.
Collection of Eileen S. Kaminsky
PLATE 37

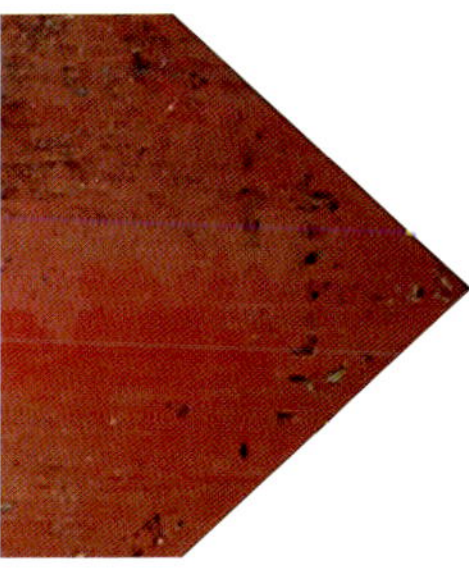

Gerhard Richter
(German, b. 1932)
Abstract Picture (Rhombus) (851-1), 1998
Oil on canvas, 90¼ x 101⅛ in.
The Museum of Fine Arts, Houston; Gift of Caroline Wiess Law in honor of Peter C. Marzio, Director, the Museum of Fine Arts, Houston
PLATE 38

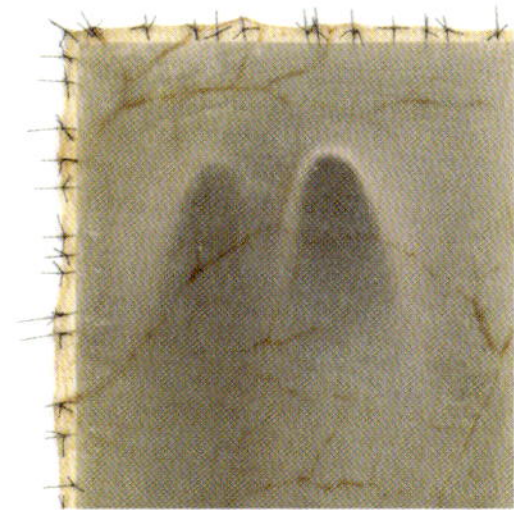

Doris Salcedo
(Colombian, b. 1958)
Atrabiliarios, 1992–93
Drywall, shoes, cow bladder, and surgical thread, 35¾ x 48 x 5 in.
Collection of Diane and Bruce Halle
PLATE 39

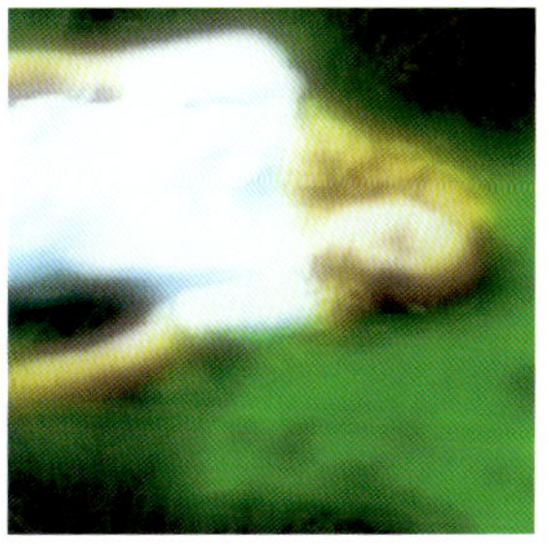

Annelies Štrba
(Swiss, b. 1947)
Frances and the Elves, 2003
DVD, 13 minutes, 4 seconds
Courtesy of the artist and Jason McCoy Gallery
PLATE 40

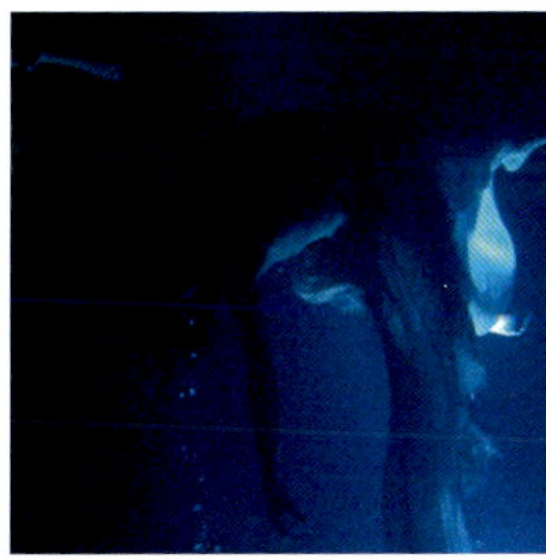

Bill Viola
(American, b. 1951)
Isolde's Ascension (The Shape of Light in Space After Death), 2005
Color high-definition on plasma display mounted on wall with stereo sound; 10 minutes, 30 seconds
Performer: Sarah Steben
Courtesy of Bill Viola Studio
PLATE 41

Page numbers in **bold** indicate illustrations.

Photo Credits

Pl. 1, Reproduced with permission of the artist
Pl. 2, © Barry X Ball
Pl. 3, © Ross Bleckner, Courtesy of Mary Boone Gallery, New York
Pl. 4, © Christian Boltanski
Pls. 5 and 6, © Janet Cardiff and George Bures Miller
Pls. 7, 8, 9, and 10, © Adam Fuss
Pls. 11, 12, and 13, © Ken Gonzales-Day
Pl. 14, © Alicia Henry
Pl. 15, © Damien Hirst and Science Ltd. All rights reserved, DACS 2015, Photo: Gareth Winters
Pl. 16, © Shirazeh Houshiary
Pl. 17, © Anish Kapoor
Pl. 18, © Elizabeth King and Richard Kizu-Blair
Pl. 19, © Elizabeth King
Pls. 20, 21, 22, 23, 24, and 25, © Deborah Luster
Pls. 26, 27, and 28, © Sally Mann
Pl. 29, © Teresa Margolles
Pl. 30, © Teresa Margolles, Image: Bridgeman Images
Pl. 31, © The Estate of Ana Mendieta Collection
Pl. 32, © The Estate of Ana Mendieta Collection, Digital images © 2015 Museum Associates/LACMA. Licensed by Art Resource, NY
Pl. 33, 34, 35, and 36, © Shirin Neshat
Pl. 37, © Hermann Nitsch, Image: courtesy of Mike Weiss Gallery, New York
Pl. 38, © Gerhard Richter 2015
Pl. 39, © Doris Salcedo
Pl. 40, © Annelies Štrba
Pl. 41, © Bill Viola Studio, Photos: Kira Perov